FAMOUS SHIPS OF WORLD WAR 2

FAMOUS SHIPS OF WORLD WAR 2
IN COLOUR

by

Chris Ellis

illustrated by

JOHN W. WOOD
J. PELLING
B. HILEY
W. HOBSON

ARCO PUBLISHING COMPANY, INC.
New York

Published 1977 by Arco Publishing Company, Inc.
219 Park Avenue South, New York, N.Y. 10003

Copyright © Blandford Press Ltd 1976

Printed in Great Britain

Library of Congress Cataloging in Publication Data

Ellis, Chris.
  Famous ships of World War 2.

  (Arco color series)
  Includes index.
    1. Warships.   2. Merchant ships.   3. World War,
1939–1945—Naval operations.   I. Title.
V767.E44   1977   940.54'59   76-52987
ISBN 0-668-04225-7
ISBN 0-668-04231-1 pbk.

CONTENTS

CONTENTS

INTRODUCTION

This book follows the style of Laurence Dunn's *Merchant Ships of the World in Colour 1910-29* and was originally going to be restricted to warships only. However, the title was broadened to include some mercantile ships or ships of merchant origin, since both world wars saw sea warfare become a 'total' conflict, above, on, and below the ocean, and any ship at sea was likely to get involved in some aspect of hostilities, including the most innocent of neutrals. Modern sea warfare is uncompromisingly hostile, for apart from the hazards of shot, shell, torpedo, and bomb there is the common enemy of all ships and mariners, the sea and the weather, which can kill and destroy even when weapons fail to do so.

In a conflict as long as World War 2, six years of intense naval activity involved ships of virtually every maritime nation. Actions took place in almost every sea and ocean of the world, though the really intense fighting was in the Atlantic, Mediterranean, and Pacific. Naval strengths were built up on a vast scale, unlikely to be surpassed in future, by the United States and Great Britain and the lesser participants, with only the Soviet Union in the 1960s and 1970s building up a naval and merchant fleet bigger than ever before. This book presents a selection of the ships and types of ship which fought in the greatest of all wars, the 1939-45 period.

The most difficult work in the preparing of this book was selecting the subjects. An initial listing of ships which could be considered 'famous' in the sense of celebrated and renowned worked out about five times longer than the final choice. A ruthless pruning of the initial listing still left about twice as many ships as the size of the book would allow. Bearing in mind the nature of the series, with colour illustrations and an international readership, a final selection was made which had regard to a balance reflecting very roughly the naval strengths of the participants in World War 2, and a visual contrast between types and colour schemes. If we stuck to the definition of 'famous' already noted, many types of ship would not be included at all. But there were a good many classes and types of both warship and merchant ship in World War 2 which were little known to the public by name but were of the greatest importance in maritime terms. Few laymen, for instance, could name an actual Liberty Ship or a Destroyer Escort as a famous ship, yet these were just two of the types crucial to the Allied war effort. Thus some of the names of ships in this book might be completely unknown to the reader not already familiar with naval affairs in detail, but the types or classes they represent are all of considerable importance. The space considerations have meant some omissions which, in this volume at least, are unavoidable. Hence landing craft, British destroyers and submarines, and some other types are missing altogether. On the other hand there are some cases where more than one ship of similar type is shown since it is useful to indicate by means of the colour plates how very different ships could look when in alternative colour schemes or only slightly altered.

Unlike in the fields of aircraft and military uniforms, research into World War 2 colour schemes for ships is still, at the time of writing, in relative infancy. For some navies a good deal of documentation has been discovered and recorded, while for other navies almost nothing has been unearthed, though a good deal can be deduced from the study of photographs. In this book the colour schemes shown have been verified as closely as possible by author and artist either from known documentation, from war-time colour photographs (in very few cases), or else by deduction or interpretation from half-tone photographs. Any comments or additional information from readers would be welcomed, care of the publishers.

One thing that will be apparent from a glance at the colour pages, however, is that a bleak neutral grey of no memorable shade was by no means the universal colour for warships in World War 2. Greys, blues, greens, white, black, pink, and browns were all to be seen on warships (and merchantmen to a lesser extent) as attempts at concealment or confusion were tried, altered, superseded, and in some instances abandoned altogether.

It is impossible in a small volume like this to list all ships in a class, to give highly detailed technical specifications, or to explain in great detail the workings and armament of a warship. A glossary of terms and abbreviations used in this book is included, however, and the basic details (where known) are given for each ship described. For more purely technical information and class lists the reader is referred to the several books on navies of World War 2 wherein can be found particulars of ships class by class. A summary of colour schemes is also given and where a colour scheme is identifiable it is referred to in the description of the relevant ship.

Chris Ellis

April 1976

GLOSSARY OF TERMS AND EVENTS

This section explains in brief form some of the terms and events mentioned in the descriptive text in this book.

AA Anti-aircraft.

ABDA Command Combined American–British–Dutch–Australian Command set up 15 January 1942, to meet the Japanese threat in the South-West Pacific. It lasted only six weeks during which time the Japanese over-ran the area and the Battle of the Java Sea took place.

Asdic Name for anti-submarine detection equipment based on sound ranging under water. Taken from 'Anti-Submarine Detection Investigation Committee', the body which first evaluated the idea. This was the British term for what was more commonly known as Sonar.

Battles

Coral Sea, 6–9 May 1942; first battle where surface vessels of the opposing fleets (Japan, America) did not make contact, all action being by carrier aircraft.

Java Sea, 27–28 February 1942; attempt by ABDA forces to turn back Japanese task forces escorting troop transports for the invasion of Java. Resulted in total defeat for ABDA ships.

Marianas, 13–20 June 1944; greatest action by U.S. Navy against the Japanese, included Battle of the Philippine Sea. Largest ever U.S. carrier task force (TF 58) destroyed over 300 Japanese aircraft and sank many ships in 'The Great Marianas Turkey Shoot'.

Midway, 3–7 June 1942; another carrier aircraft battle which was a turning point in favour of the U.S. Navy in the Pacific.

Okinawa, March–June 1945; massive sea, air, and amphibious operation to capture an important island which would give a good base for attacking Japan itself.

River Plate, 13–17 December 1939; action between three British cruisers (*Exeter*, *Achilles*, *Ajax*) and 'pocket battleship' *Graf Spee* off Montevideo, resulting in scuttling of the trapped German ship.

Solomons: series of battles in a 1942 campaign which included Guadalcanal, Cape Esperance, Santa Cruz to keep the Japanese from over-running the entire Solomons Islands chain. Solomons campaign continued into 1943.

Bofors Swedish design of 40 mm (2 pdr), quick-firing AA gun widely produced and used by the U.S. Navy, and later the Royal Navy.

Boot topping The edging to underwater colouring at the waterline.

Canadian Maritime Commission Canadian body supervising the building and running of Canadian merchant service and its ships.

Catapult Also known as an accelerator (U.S.). In World War 2 these were usually hydraulically operated. In cruisers and capital ships (and a few destroyers) catapults were most usually trained to a suitable direction for launching aircraft. In aircraft carriers catapults were built into the flight deck (sometimes the hangar deck) fixed relative to the ship's axis. Aircraft were launched by trolley running in the catapult track, but were later launched by a shoe to which they were attached by a wire strop.

Conning Tower In a submarine the name for the superstructure from which it is commanded while on the surface. In a large surface vessel the name for the superstructure (often armoured) which included the navigating bridge, admiral's bridge, etc.

Corvette Type name given to a small anti-submarine vessel built by the British – a revival of an eighteenth-century name.

DE Destroyer Escort (U.S. Navy type).

Decks Variously described depending on country. First fully continuous deck was usually called the main deck, and the other decks had relative names, e.g., lower deck, forecastle deck, shelter deck. U.S. Navy introduced a numbering scheme in which the main deck was '1 deck' and decks below were numbered in order '2', '3', etc. Decks above '1 deck' were numbered '01', '02', '03', etc.

Dimensions Beam = width of ship; draught (or draft) = depth of ship below water line (sometimes qualified as 'mean' or 'deep load'); length = overall (OA), water line (WL), or between perpendiculars (PP).

Director Control Tower Name for the structure (usually traversing), which contained the rangefinders, gunnery radar aerials, etc., used for ranging and directing the guns. All but small units usually had more than one DCT. There might be a DCT for forward main armament, another for aft main armament, and one or two each side for secondary armament.

Displacement Expressed as *standard* – complete ship without fuel or stores – or *full load* – ship completed stored and fuelled.

Escort Carrier Light type of aircraft carrier, mostly built on merchant type hull, or suitably converted. Some were purpose-built, however. Of slow speed they were originally intended for convoy escort work but were later used in offensive roles, especially in support of amphibious operations.

Fighting French Alternative (and more correct) term for Free French (qv).

Flag Superior Term for the key letter (e.g., L, F) carried in front of a pendant number. The upper (superior) flag therefore when the pendant number was hoisted as a flag signal.

Fleet Term for a major integrated command, usually a balanced force of ships (e.g., Atlantic Fleet).

Flotilla Term variously used in different navies for a small force of ships under command, normally of the same type, and generally used in connection with destroyers or smaller types.

Free French French forces who served under the command of General de Gaulle subsequent to the fall of France in June 1940.

Greenock A major assembly point and dispersal point in Britain for Atlantic convoys and also Russian convoys.

Halifax A major assembly and dispersal point in Canada for Atlantic convoys.

Hangar In aircraft carriers the hangar normally took up all or part of the main deck below the flight deck and this was known as the hangar deck. Intermediate decks running each side of the hangar between hangar deck and flight deck levels were known as gallery decks. A few carriers had a second hangar deck above or below the main one. The hangars were served by lifts (or elevators) usually on the centre line but at the deck edge in some U.S. ships.

Heavy Cruiser In Washington Treaty terms, a cruiser with an armament of 8-inch guns and not exceeding 10,000 tons displacement.

Hedgehog Ahead throwing anti-submarine weapon firing a pattern of twenty-four spigot-type charges, usually mounted forward of bridge. A useful supplement to depth charges in the Allied fight against German submarines.

Hull number In the U.S. Navy (and some other navies) an alternative identifying system to the pendant number. Each ship within a type grouping gets a number. Thus there may be more than one ship with the same number (e.g., battleship, carrier, destroyer, submarine, etc., each numbered 24).

K-gun U.S. Navy term for a depth charge thrower.
Knot Nautical mile per hour.

Light Cruiser In Washington Treaty terms a cruiser with main armament of 6-inch calibre or less, irrespective of ship size.

LL Sweep Electric impulse minesweeping gear for dealing with magnetic mines. Usually in the form of a long insulated loop of cable stowed aft on a prominent drum.

London Naval Treaty Treaty of 1930 which limited the relative strengths of the main naval powers, notably Britain, U.S.A. and Japan.

O Sweep Oropesa sweep gear for moored contact mines, with float, 'kite', and cutting wire. Usually stowed prominently aft in minesweepers with prominent davits for handling the equipment.

Oerlikon Swiss arms factory whose 20 mm quick-firing cannon was widely adopted and used by the Allies; in single and twin mounts in U.S. and British ships.

8

Panzerschiffe German 'armoured ship' – the designation given to the small, heavily armoured 'miniature battleships' of the *Graf Spee* type built by Germany in the 1930s.

Paravane Specialised sweeping gear for severing moored contact mines and carried by destroyers and above for self-protection. Streamed from the bows but in practice rarely used in World War 2.

Pendant Number Tactical number allocated to a particular ship for identification purposes. Not necessarily displayed on the ship's side.

Pocket Battleship Popular English term for German Panzerschiffe.

Pom-Pom Quick-firing gun, the name descriptive of the sound. In Britain it was commonly used to describe the standard Royal Navy multi-barrel 2 pdr AA gun, but in the U.S. Navy it was similarly used to describe a multi-barrel 1·1 inch AA machine gun.

Port Left side looking forward.

Quad 40 mm Popular name for very effective U.S. Navy Mk 2 Bofors mount with four guns (two twins on a common mount). Widely fitted in destroyers and above.

Radar Radio detection and ranging equipment. Associated aerials on masts and gunnery control equipment were increasingly prominent in the 1944–45 period.

Replenishment Common term for the supply of warships at sea from storeships and tankers. Latterly was usually carried out while the ships were underway.

Scapa Flow Important British fleet anchorage in the Orkneys.

Sheer The sweep of a ship's hull lines relative to the waterline or horizontal.

shp Shaft horsepower.

Sonar Sound impulse and receiving gear for underwater detection of submarines (U.S. term originally).

Squadron Term variously used by different navies for a small group of ships under command, usually of the same type (e.g., cruiser squadron).

9

Task Force Group of ships assigned to a specific tactical role, not necessarily of permanent composition. Originally a U.S. term but subsequently widely adopted. Sub-divided if necessary into Task Groups and Task Units (e.g., TF 17, TG 17.1, TU 17.1.3).

Tokyo Express U.S. Navy nickname for the night runs to supply troops and stores to the Japanese garrison on the Solomon Islands in 1942 when the Japanese forces were hard pressed by U.S. warships and marines.

Turret Strictly speaking a fully enclosed armoured gun house on an armoured barbette containing shell hoists, etc., but often loosely used to describe any enclosed mounting as in a destroyer.

Type Designator Code used by U.S. Navy (later used by others) in conjunction with hull number to fully identify a ship (e.g., *DE* 760). Some codes were: BB – battleship, PT – patrol torpedo boat, CA – heavy cruiser, CL – light cruiser, DD – destroyer, AM – minesweeper, CV – aircraft carrier, CVL – light aircraft carrier, CVE – escort aircraft carrier. There were many others.

UP Unrotating projectile (i.e., rocket), early British term.

USMC (I) United States Maritime Commission – administered merchant service. (II) United States Marine Corps.

Washington Treaty 1921 agreement by U.S.A., Great Britain, France, Italy, and Japan to limit tonnages of ships (e.g., battleships 35,000 tons) and ratio of size of naval force between the nations based on 5 : 5 : 3 proportion for America, Britain and Japan with France and Italy a 1·75 ratio of that. Included also a ten-year 'holiday' in capital ship building.

WAR-TIME COLOUR SCHEMES

Since the early part of the twentieth century, grey in some shade or other has been adopted by most navies as a utilitarian colour in which warships can be painted. In the nineteenth century and earlier when naval wars were more leisurely affairs and weapons were of short range there was little attempt at concealing ships from enemy observation. Typical nineteenth-century warship colours, in the days of sail, and carried over into the first decades of steam, were black or white and buff, 'easy' paints to mix, apply, and keep clean. Prior to the World War I grey had come into almost universal use among warships of the world, in itself a form of concealment camouflage for it has been proved that in average weather conditions a grey painted ship is less conspicuous than a ship in almost any other colour. It was realised from the start that it is virtually impossible to completely conceal a ship on the open sea. In certain conditions of light and sea surface it may not be obviously visible at a first casual glance. But enemy ships would be keeping a vigilant watch around the horizon.

In World War I it became a popular idea to forget about *conceal-ment* completely and aim instead to *confuse* the enemy. This led to the idea of 'dazzle' painting, using contrasting colours in bold patterns which broke up the outline of a ship and made it difficult for a submarine commander to judge the course and distance of his target ship through his periscope, or for a rangefinder operator to find an exact point of focus. In 'dazzle' painting such devices as false bows or sterns (sometimes at the 'wrong' ends) were favourite tricks. Other visual tricks evolved in the World War I period included 'painting out', say, two funnels of a four funnel ship in light colours (e.g., white), and painting the other two a dark shade; from a distance the white funnels would 'disappear' against the skyline while the dark funnels would be prominent, thus giving at first sighting the impression of a two funnel ship and so making identification difficult without closer study of the target. The false bow wave painted in white at the forefoot was a very early trick – some British battleships at the Dardanelles used it. To the distant observer a stationary ship gives the impression of movement while a moving ship may appear to be moving faster than it really is.

By 1918 the U.S. Navy, Royal Navy, and German Navy were all using 'dazzle' and confusion painting to some degree, and a good deal of research had been done into the subject. In the inter-war period the navies went back, without exception, to plain grey shades, easy and cheap to apply and a happy compromise. In the 1930s the U.S. Navy in particular did a lot of research into colour or camouflage schemes for warships, and by 1940 when war was already declared in Europe, the U.S. Navy Bureau of Ships introduced a number of standardised colour schemes based on research (some of which drew on World War 1 experience). Other navies seem to have done much less formal work on colour schemes between the wars; by way of example British records show that when various individual ship captains were commending or reporting on suggested camouflage schemes in 1939–40, there was some confusion as to which department of the Admiralty should take responsibility for examining or authorising the suggested schemes.

Once the war started, however, virtually all the major navies either developed or adapted the standard peace-time colours to war conditions, or produced more elaborate confusion or concealment schemes. Irrespective of nation, it soon became generally realised that very light colours offered the best concealment value, even in the dark, and dark colours made a vessel too prominent – thus a black ship at night tended to show up more than a light grey one, so all-black colour schemes were generally short-lived in any navy. Despite the appearance of radar and the wide use of aircraft at sea, camouflage was by no means outdated. Much sea fighting took place still with a big reliance on visual sighting, as in the case of a submarine attack. And it was proved possible in some instances to confuse reconnaissance aircraft or reduce the visibility of a surface target by certain paint schemes.

Tactical markings

In addition to ordinary camouflage painting, there was one area in which a limited degree of conspicuous painting was required. A force commander of any sort of naval formation (flotilla, squadron, convoy escort group, task force) requiring to exercise tactical control over ships in company could rely on quick indentification by codes painted on the sides or in some other prominent position of the ships. Different countries had different systems and in many navies, large units (say cruisers and above) did not carry these tactical codes – known as pendant (or pennant) numbers, or hull numbers, depending on the navy. Some navies, notably the U.S., had code letters designating the ship type, while others had a letter (e.g., F) indicating a classification or group and preceding the number. In general these tactical numbers were painted prominently in peace-time but in a much smaller size, or a less conspicuous colour in war-time. Small ships operating in flotillas or squadrons often used some type of number or symbol, frequently on the funnel, as an identifier. This could be almost any sort of sign, a number, a geometrical shape, or a cartoon character, its significance not necessarily having any meaning to the outsider.

Other colours
Certain other colours and markings could be seen, not necessarily concerned with camouflage. In some navies life-saving equipment, such as cork rafts, were brightly painted; the Royal Navy used red and yellow quarters on Carley floats in the latter half of the war, though not on all ships, mainly in fact on convoy escorts where the risk of a ship being torpedoed and having to launch the rafts was greater. Lifeboats were sometimes furnished with brightly coloured cloth panels for a similar reason, the panel being spread out over the boat to assist any searching aircraft.

Hospital ships and some relief ships were painted to conform to Geneva Convention requirements, white with red crosses and a green stripe round the hull was the most common scheme. Ships of neutral powers engaged in trading normally had their name and country of origin painted very prominently on the sides, with a national flag also displayed or painted. On occasion ships of the fighting powers used this type of marking as a ruse to escape detection or catch the enemy; *Altmark* and her sister ships were adept at this sort of trick early in the war. To change the appearance of a ship, also, sheets of canvas, dummy guns, and canvas 'baffles' suspended between funnels were used on a number of occasions.

Recognition by colour from the air was yet another frequent necessity for the benefit of friendly forces; the German Navy were noted users of this sort of scheme. For a certain operation turret tops of one ship might be pink, another yellow, and so on. For the next operation all the colours would be changed. The Japanese favoured the national flag as an air identifier for friendly aircraft. Most aircraft carriers – certainly American ones – had a deck identifying number, while numbers or markings on turret tops were common in most navies, usually for specific operations. Ships of the Neutrality Patrol off Spain in the 1937–39 period had stripes in national colours round turrets or parts of the superstructure; the ships of Vichy France continued this practice later and the battleship *Strasbourg* is shown so marked in this book.

Some more detailed notes of specific camouflage schemes used by the main fighting powers are given below. In general the notes are confined to schemes which are specifically illustrated in this book.

U.S. Navy

By 1940 the U.S. Navy had put a very comprehensive series of specific camouflage schemes into operation, well over twenty being in use at various times. There were many 'unofficial' variations or interpretations of official schemes.

MEASURE 1: Dark grey overall, usually with all masts and tops above bridge level painted white for low visibility when hull down. This was mostly used in the 1940–41 period.

MEASURE 2: Dark grey hull, light grey upperworks. Sometimes white or pale grey on masts and high on superstructure. For a good example see *Reuben James* in this book.

MEASURE 4: All black – little used for reasons stated above.

MEASURE 5: False bow wave painted with any other scheme.

MEASURE 7/MEASURE 8: Deceptive designs whereby cruisers were painted to resemble destroyers.

MEASURE 11: A solid colour system, sea blue overall. This was used in the Pacific and Mediterranean and tended to render ships fairly inconspicuous from the air. Decks were also painted this colour.

MEASURE 12: This was an early (1942) system of toning a ship into the sea. Navy blue or dark grey was used low on the hull, was blended in mottle fashion with ocean grey at about main deck level, and this in turn was blended with haze grey or pale grey on the superstructure sides. See *Hornet (I)* and *Nicholas* for examples.

MEASURE 13: Haze grey overall. Introduced in some ships during the war and retained post-war. See *Robert E. Keller* in this book. Haze grey was found to be the best 'compromise' colour for all average conditions.

MEASURE 14: Overall ocean grey. A utilitarian colour used on much war-time construction, usually applied overall. Also used on U.S. Maritime Commission ships. See *Franklin* and *Patrick Henry* for examples.

MEASURE 16: This was a revived World War I system of white with a pattern of light sea blue, known as the Thayer System, and was used extensively in the North Atlantic. In some light conditions the white could render a ship almost invisible against the skyline. See *Surprise* as an example.

MEASURE 21: A later variation of 11, using navy blue instead of sea blue and used quite frequently late in the war.

MEASURE 22: This became the commonest scheme. From a given low point, usually the lowest point of the first continuous deck, the lower hull was painted navy blue, and all above was haze grey. The navy blue merged well with the sea and it became difficult at any distance to judge the ship's position relative to the horizon.

MEASURE 31: A dark pattern system using greens, browns, and greys, much used on landing craft and PT boats operating inshore in the Pacific.

MEASURE 32: A medium 'dazzle' system using navy blue, haze grey, pale grey, ocean grey, or equivalent greens. See *Hornet (II)* for a good example.

MEASURE 33: As above but using only lighter tones, pale grey, haze grey, ocean grey, or equivalent greens. See *Nashville* and *West Point* for examples. Used in the North Pacific and North Atlantic.

Standard colour for all decks and horizontal surfaces was deck blue (a blue grey shade), but other colours were often substituted. On carrier decks, dark grey, deck blue, sea blue, or navy blue might be used. Hull numbers were small and unblocked, carried on all ships at bow and stern, and on island side in carriers. In peace-time, large white blocked hull numbers were used.

Royal Navy (Great Britain)

In peace-time, RN ships were generally dark grey in home waters, light grey in the Mediterranean or southern latitudes, and, sometimes, white with buff funnels in the Middle and Far East. In 1939–40 a number of 'free-lance' camouflage schemes appeared on some ships, mostly similar to the dazzle patterns of World War 1, but there were others.

WESTERN APPROACHES SCHEME: This was a 'free-lance' scheme first put forward by the artist/naturalist Peter Scott, similar in concept to the American Thayer Scheme. An all white ship with panels of light sea blue or light sea green proved a good combination for the North Atlantic, the white merging with the skyline in average weather conditions, the other colours with the sea. It was accepted as an official scheme in 1941 and was widely used – see *Aconit* and *Alisma*.

MOUNTBATTEN PINK: Devised by Lord Mountbatten, this was a mix of some red paint with light grey to give a pinkish effect. Camouflage experts disagreed with its value, for in some conditions it could show up darker. It was popular, but never official.

ADMIRALTY DISRUPTIVE PATTERNS (LIGHT, INTERMEDIATE, DARK): These were true camouflage patterns using multi-colours in lobed patterns, differing port and starboard and individual to each ship. For an example of the Dark scheme see *Howe* and for the Intermediate scheme see *Illustrious*. The Light scheme was similar to the Western Approaches scheme, but less angular in pattern. These patterns were mostly used in 1942–44. A special range of blues and greys and greens, all coded, were produced for use with these Disruptive patterns.

HOME FLEET DESTROYER SCHEME: Unique to destroyers this had light patterns forward (similar to the Western Approaches Scheme) and darker colours (blues or greys) aft.

ADMIRALTY STANDARD SCHEMES: This replaced the disruptive schemes from 1944 and was much simpler. The Standard Scheme featured a sea blue panel on an overall light grey hull, the panel stretching from the forward to after guns. The panel had a foreshortening effect. In some ships the panel was taken from right forward to right aft.

ADMIRALTY ALTERNATIVE SCHEME: Dark grey hull, light grey upperworks. Widely used in the Mediterranean. It had rather the same optical effect as the U.S. Navy's MEASURE 22. In many cases Royal Navy ships remained plain light grey (e.g., *Inman*), or dark grey (e.g., *Furious*). Pendant numbers on destroyers and below were usually red, blue, white, or black, showing to sides and stern. Decks were usually painted (or stained) dark grey.

German Navy

Pre-war German ships were painted either light grey overall or light grey with dark grey hulls. The funnel cowl, or sometimes the entire funnel was in some ships graphited for insulation purposes, giving a 'silver-grey' effect. Many ships retained these colours in war-time, though the graphiting of the funnel was discontinued. Decks in wartime were painted very dark grey. A very pale grey (almost white) shade was used extensively in the war years, specially on small ships (e.g., *S-10*). Some camouflage combinations, typically a 'splinter' or dazzle pattern, were introduced and these sometimes involved 'painting out' the bow and stern. Pale grey, dark grey, and sea blue were typical combinations (see *Schleswig-Holstein*). On large units (see *Prinz Eugen*) schemes were used to 'paint out' bows and stern and give bold vertical contrasts to confuse rangefinders.

There were many 'free-lance' schemes. The well documented history of the *Graf Spee* shows that the camouflage she had at the River Plate – false bow wave and wash, disruptive pattern on superstructure – appeared to be the idea of the captain. Some S-Boats and other small craft had multi-hued mottled finishes with pinks, blues, greens, etc., over the basic pale light grey. U-Boats were mostly dark grey overall, but many had light grey superstructures, and some had pale grey with dark grey disruptive patterns, like small surface vessels. Some torpedo boats were black early in the war.

Italian Navy

The peace-time colour of light grey overall remained in use in 1940–43, but most major vessels were given 'splinter' type disruptive schemes featuring dark grey, light sea blue, light sea green, and light grey. *Andrea Doria* and *Vittorio Veneto* are typical; each big ship had its own unique pattern. A distinctive air recognition device was used. The foredeck of each ship was painted in alternate diagonal stripes of white and bright red.

Japanese Navy

The pre-war colour of dark grey (which had a distinct blueish tinge) was retained. Pre-war ships had the name painted in prominent letters amidships, but this was discontinued when war broke out. Some cruisers were given a disruptive pattern by applying very pale grey over the dark grey (e.g., *Myoko*) but few other types of ship appear to have been so painted. A dark sea green was applied to some major units, notably aircraft carriers but also to some other types (see *Junyo*). Decks were dark grey; some carriers had decks painted in the various colours to break up the slab-like outline.

Soviet Navy

Dark grey overall, or dark grey with medium grey upperworks (e.g., *Kirov*) were the most common war-time colours. Boot topping red or black, sometimes with a white line. There is little evidence of any disruptive patterns being used, at least on any wide scale.

French Navy

Pre-war French ships were light grey and those ships interned or in Vichy hands in 1940 remained so painted. Ships which joined the Fighting (Free) French in 1940 adopted Royal Navy colours and camouflage (e.g., *Aconit*). Ships refitted in the U.S.A. were invariably returned to service in a colour scheme equivalent to U.S. Navy MEA-SURE 22. Distinctive features of all French ships were the black-painted anchors. There were exceptions – *Béarn* was in U.S. Navy MEASURE 33 for North Atlantic service, as were some small French ships.

Lease-Lend Ships

Ships supplied to Allied navies from the U.S.A. were most commonly painted in a suitable U.S. Navy colour which was usually retained, at least for a while by the new owner (e.g., *Hova*, *AM. 142*, *Ameer*).

Merchant Ships

The British Ministry of War Transport suggested standard dark and light greys for hull and upperworks respectively, but some British owners went their own way. A few were dazzle painted, masts were grey of some sort: one line had sky blue top masts. The Canadian Maritime Commission suggested light grey with white topmasts, and the U.S. Maritime Commission specified overall ocean gray.

n.b. Diagrams illustrating applications of camouflage patterns are given on page 205.

THE COLOUR PLATES

1. Patrick Henry, Liberty Ship, U.S.A., 1941.
10,805 tons (gross), 11 knots, 441½ × 57 × 27 ft.
First 'Liberty' class dry cargo ship completed. Typical of the type supplied to the British, Soviet, and U.S. merchant marines. Standard Ocean Gray colour.

2. Ocean Liberty, Ocean PF/Ship, U.S.A./U.K., 1942.
7,174 tons (gross), 11 knots, 441¼ × 57 ft, 1 × 4 inch.
First 'Ocean' type emergency war freighter of a total of 60 built in United States yards,
1941-42, for the British Ministry War Transport. Coal burning.

3.- **Fort Wallace, North Sands Ship, Canada/U.K., 1944.**
7,150 tons (gross), 11 knots, 441½×57 ft, 2×2 pdr, 2×20 mm.
'Victory' type standard dry cargo vessel, built in Canada, one of a total of 90 supplied Lend-Lease to the British government. De-gaussing equipment fitted.

4. Kirov, Cruiser, U.S.S.R., 1940.
8,800 tons, 35 knots, 626¾ × 59 × 20 ft,
9 × 7.1 inch, 8 × 4 inch, 6 × 13 mm.
Appearance as in the Baltic Fleet for Russo-
Finnish War, late 1940. *Inset.* Russian
Naval Ensign.

5. Oktyabrskaya Revolutsia, Battleship, U.S.S.R., 1941.
23,606 tons, 23 knots, 619×87×27½ ft, 12×12 inch, 12×4.7 inch, 8×3 inch, 12×37 mm.

Shown as painted at the outbreak of the war with Germany, 1941.

6. Leningrad, Destroyer, U.S.S.R., 1941.
2,225 tons, 38 knots, 418½ × 38½ × 13 ft, 4 × 5.1 inch, 2 × 3 inch, 5 × 37 mm. Shown as painted early in the war. *Inset.* Russian naval 'jack'.

7. AM.142, Minesweeper, U.S.A./U.S.S.R., 1943.
650 tons, 16 knots, 184½ × 33 × 10 ft, 1 × 3 inch, 2 × 40 mm, 6 × 20 mm.
Shown on delivery to Soviet Union, 1943. One of a total of 34 supplied under Lend-Lease. Measure 22 camouflage.

8. Shtshuka class, Submarine, U.S.S.R., 1942.
620/738 tons, 15½/8½ knots, 190¼ × 19¼ × 13 ft, 1 × 45 mm, 6 × 21 inch torpedo tubes.
Appearance as in 1942; some boats had a second 45 mm gun.

9. Maluitka class, Coastal Submarine, U.S.S.R., 1940.
205/256 tons, 13/7 knots, 146 × 10¼ × 8½ ft, 1 × 45 mm, 2 × 21 inch torpedo tubes.
'M' class pre-fabricated small submarine. Later type illustrated.

10. **Georges Leygues, Light Cruiser, France, 1945.**
1,600 tons, 31 knots, 581 × 57½ × 17½ ft, 9 × 6 inch, 8 × 3.5 inch, 6 × 40 mm, 16 × 20mm.
Shown after refit in U.S.A. with major alterations.

11. Strasbourg, Battleship, France, 1940.

26,500 tons, 31½ knots, 702 × 101 ft, 8 × 13 inch, 16 × 5.1 inch, 8 × 37 mm, 32 × 13.2 mm.

Shown in Mediterranean in 1940 with French national markings. *Inset.* Loire 130 flying boat carried by *Strasbourg.*

12. Richelieu, Battleship, France, 1944.
35,000 tons, 32 knots, $813\frac{1}{2} \times 116\frac{1}{4} \times 30$ ft, 8×15 inch, 12×4 inch, 60×40 mm, 50×20 mm.
Shown in British Admiralty standard camouflage scheme while serving with the British Eastern Fleet in July 1944.

13. Bearn, Aircraft Carrier, France, 1944.

18,000 tons, 21 knots, 593 × 114 ft, 4 × 5 inch, 6 × 40 mm, 20 × 20 mm.
Shown in 1944 in service as an aircraft transport after completion of major refit and re-arming in U.S.A. Painted to U.S. Navy Measure 33.

14. Le Fantasque, Destroyer, France, 1944.
2,569 tons, 37 knots, 435 × 40¼ × 16¼ ft, 5 × 5.5 inch, 4 × 37 mm, 4 × 13.2 mm, 9 × 21.7 mm torpedo tubes.
Shown painted to U.S. Navy Measure 22 on completion of refit in U.S.A., early 1944.

15. Aconit, Corvette, U.K./France, 1942.
925 tons, 16 knots, 205 × 33 × 11½ ft, 1 × 4 inch, 2 × 2 pdr.
'Flower' class, ex-Royal Navy. Long forecastle type. Western Approaches colour scheme.

16. Hova, Destroyer Escort, U.S.A./France, 1944.
1,240 tons, 21 knots, 306 × 36¼ × 8¼ ft, 3 × 3 inches, 1 × 40 mm, 18 × 20 mm.
'Cannon' class DE, ex- U.S. Navy. Painted to Measure 22 shown as in 1944.

17. Surcouf, Corsair Submarine, France, 1940.
3,304/4,218 tons, 18/8¼ knots, 360 × 29 ft, 2 × 8 inch, 2 × 37 mm, 6 × 21.7 inch torpedo
tubes, 4 × 18 inch torpedo tubes.
Shown immediately pre-war with Besson MB.411 floatplane embarked.

18. Rubis, Minelaying Submarine, France, 1940.
761/925 tons, 12/9 knots, 214¼ × 23¼ × 13¼ ft, 1 × 13.2 mm, 1 × 75 mm, 3 × 21.7 inch
torpedo tubes, 2 × 15.7 inch torpedo tubes, 32 mines.
Shown in 1940 at time of joining Free French naval forces. *Inset.* French national ensign.

19. Andrea Doria, Battleship, Italy, 1943.
22,964 tons, 27 knots, 612 × 92 × 30 ft, 12 × 12.6 inch, 12 × 5.2 inch, 10 × 3.5 inch, 19 × 37 mm.
One of four fully reconstructed vessels, originally built 1913-14. Camouflage scheme shown as carried at time of Italian Armistice in September 1943.

20. Bartolomeo Colleoni class, Light Cruisers, Italy, 1940–42.
5,100 tons, 37 knots, 555 × 51 × 16¼ ft, 4 × 6 inch, 6 × 3.9 inch, 2 × 21 inch torpedo tubes.
Bande Nere shown as camouflaged just before being sunk by British submarine, March
1942. *Bartolomeo Colleoni* was plain light grey, as 'Zara' (plate 21).

21. Zara, Heavy Cruiser, Italy, 1941.
10,000 tons, 32 knots, 620 × 68 × 19¼ ft,
8 × 8 inch, 12 × 3.9 inch, 8 × 37 mm,
8 × 13.2 mm.
Colour scheme shown as at Battle of
Matapan.

22. Vittorio Veneto, Battleship, Italy, 1943.
35,000 tons, 30·5 knots, 780 × 108 × 31¼ ft, 9 × 15 inch, 12 × 6 inch, 4 × 4.7 inch,
12 × 3.5 inch, 20 × 37 mm, 32 × 20 mm.
Colour scheme shown as that carried at the time of the Italian Armistice in September
1943.

23. Kongo, Battleship, Japan, 1942.
31,720 tons, 30 knots, 730 × 95¼ × 32 ft, 8 × 14 inch, 14 × 6 inch, 8 × 5 inch, 10 × 25 mm. Shown with air identification marks on turrets and white 'low visibility' director. *Inset.* Admiral's flag.

24. Yamato, Battleship, Japan, 1943.
64,170 tons, 27.5 knots, 863 × 127¼ × 35¼ ft, 9 × 18 inch, 6 × 6.1 inch, 12 × 5 inch, 87 × 25 mm, 4 × 13 mm, 6 aircraft.
Ship is shown as in 1943 with two extra triple 6.1 inch turrets, one on each beam. Catapults are sited at stern. Standard Japanese Navy grey colour scheme.

25. Akagi, Aircraft Carrier, Japan, 1939.
36,500 tons, 31 knots, 855 × 102¼ × 28¼ ft, 12 × 8 inch, 2 × 8 inch, 28 × 25 mm. Converted from battle-cruiser in 1925. Carried about 90 aircraft. Admiral Nagumo's flagship. *Inset.* Japanese national ensign.

26. Junyo, Aircraft Carrier, Japan, 1944.

24,140 tons, 25¼ knots, 719½ × 87¼ × 26¼ ft, 12 × 5 inch, 40 × 25 mm, 6 × 12 cm rocket projectors.

Converted liner altered to carrier in 1940; carried about 53 aircraft. Sister ship *Hiyo* was sunk in 1944. *Inset.* Imperial Japanese Navy ensign.

27. Myoko, Heavy Cruiser, Japan, 1944.
13,380 tons, 33¼ knots, 661¼ × 68 × 20½ ft, 10 × 8 inch, 8 × 5 inch, 8 × 25 mm, 4 × 13 mm.
Shown as camouflaged in 1944.

28. Fubuki, Destroyer, Japan, 1937.
2,090 tons, 34 knots, 388 × 34 × 10½, 4 × 5 inch, 14 × 25 mm, 9 × 24 inch torpedo tubes. Nameship of class, shown in pre-war colour scheme with name and pennant numbers displayed. *Inset.* Imperial Japanese Navy ensign.

29. Yukikaze, Destroyer, Japan, 1940.
2,033 tons, 35 knots, 388¼×35½×12½ ft,
6×5 inch, 4×25 mm, 2×13 mm, 8×24
inch torpedo tubes.
Shown as first commissioned in January
1940.

30. I-168, Cruiser Submarine (KD 6A class), 1939.
1,400/2,000 tons, 23/8 knots, 343 × 27 × 15 ft, 1 × 3·9 inch, 1 × 13 mm, 6 × 21 inch torpedo tubes (14 torpedoes).
Shown in standard finish with pennant number as 'I-68' before renumbering to 'I-168'.

31. San Demetrio, Tanker, U.K., 1940.
8,073 tons (gross), 12 knots, 463 ft long.
Eagle Oil and Shipping Co. vessel shown
on return to the Clyde, November 1940.

32. Jervis Bay, Armed Merchant Cruiser, U.K., 1940.
14,164 knots (gross), 15 knots, $548\frac{1}{4} \times 68\frac{1}{4} \times 33\frac{1}{4}$ ft, 8×6 inch, 2×3 inch.
Ex-Aberdeen and Commonwealth Lines ship, converted to AMC.

33. Sydney, Light Cruiser, Australia, 1939.
6,830 tons, 32½ knots, 555 × 56¼ × 15¾ ft, 8 × 6 inch, 8 × 4 inch, 12 × 0.5 inch, 8 × 21 inch torpedo tubes.
Shown in service in the Mediterranean in 1939 carrying British recognition markings on 'B' turret as part of the Neutrality Patrol for the Spanish Civil War.

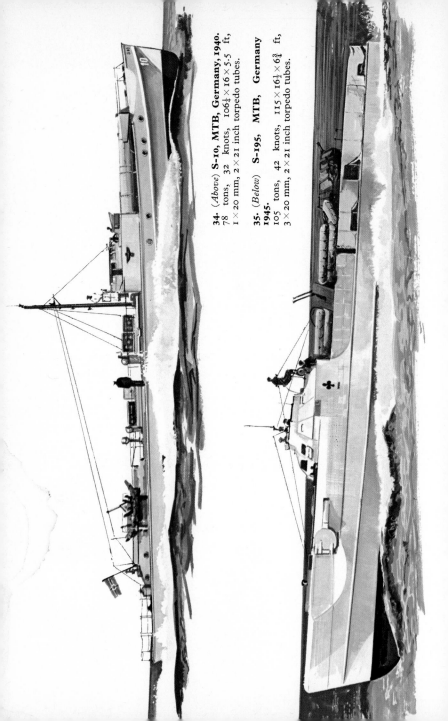

34. (*Above*) **S-10, MTB, Germany, 1940.** 78 tons, 32 knots, 106¼ × 16 × 5.5 ft, 1 × 20 mm, 2 × 21 inch torpedo tubes.

35. (*Below*) **S-195, MTB, Germany 1945.** 105 tons, 42 knots, 115 × 16¼ × 6¾ ft, 3 × 20 mm, 2 × 21 inch torpedo tubes.

36. Biber 90, Midget Submarine, Germany, 1944.

7 tons, 10/6 knots, 29½ × 3¾ × 5¼ ft, 2 × 21 inch torpedo tubes.

One-man midget submarine, of a class of over 300. This one was captured by the British; carries a typical form of decoration. *Inset.* Close-up of propeller rudder and port-side torpedo.

37. Hornet, Aircraft Carrier, U.S.A., 1942.

20,000 tons, 33 knots, 809½ × 83 × 28 ft, 8 × 5 inch, 16 × 1.1 inch, 23 × 20 mm. Measure 12 camouflage. *Inset.* B-25B Mitchell bomber used in Tokyo Raid, April 1942.

38. Illustrious, Aircraft Carrier, U.K., 1945.
31,630 tons, 30 knots, 748½ × 95¼ × 24 ft, 16 × 4.5 inch, 48 × 2 pdr, 3 × 40 mm.
52 × 20 mm.
Shown in Admiralty Disruptive camouflage scheme, after refit in U.S.A.

39. Furious, Aircraft Carrier, U.K., 1940.
22,450 tons, 28½ knots, 786¼×89¾×26 ft, 12×4 inch, 32×2 pdr.
Converted light battle-cruiser, semi-sister to *Glorious* but with smaller island and engine-room exhaust outlets aft. Shown in Admiralty grey in 1940 with stern painted black to conceal smoke staining. *Inset.* Swordfish of *Furious* carrier air group in May 1940.

40. Glorious, Aircraft Carrier, U.K., 1940.
22,450 tons, 28½ knots, 786¼ × 89¼ × 26 ft, 12 × 4 inch, 32 × 2 pdr.
Converted battle-cruiser, reconstructed as aircraft carrier 1924-30. Sunk by gunfire
when intercepted by German ships *Gneisenau* and *Scharnhorst*, 8 June 1940, near
Narvik. Colour scheme shown as in September 1939. *Inset.* Ship's badge.

41. Schleswig-Holstein, Battleship, Germany, 1942.
13,200 tons, 18 knots, 419 × 72 × 26¼ ft,
4 × 11 inch, 10 × 5·9 inch.
As camouflaged for operations in the Baltic
throughout the war.

42. Alabama, Battleship, U.S.A., 1942.
35,000 tons, 28 knots, 679¼ × 108¼ × 36¾ ft, 9 × 16 inch, 20 × 5 inch, 48 × 40 mm.
Shown in Measure 12 camouflage. *Inset.* Ship's Kingfisher aircraft (three carried).

43. Prince of Wales, Battleship, U.K., 1941.
35,000 tons, 28½ knots, 745 × 103 × 34 ft, 10 × 14 inch,
16 × 5.25 inch, 48 × 2 pdr, 1 × 40 mm, 7 × 20 mm.
Shown in first Admiralty Disruptive camouflage
scheme on sailing for the Far East late in 1941.

44. Altmark, Supply Ship, Germany, 1940.
22,500 tons (gross), 21 knots, 582 × 72½ × 30¼ ft, 3 × 15 cm, 2 × 2 cm.
Shown off Norway on return from South Atlantic station after Battle of the River Plate.

45. Java, Light Cruiser, Netherlands, 1941.

6,670 tons, 31 knots, 509¼ × 52¼ × 18 ft, 10 × 5.9 inch, 8 × 40 mm. Shown with awnings spread, on Dutch East Indies station in 1941 prior to outbreak of war in the Far East.

46. Admiral Graf Spee, Armoured Ship, Germany, 1939.
12,100 tons, 26/28 knots, 609¼ × 69½ × 21⅔ ft, 6 × 11 inch, 6 × 6 inch, 8 × 5.9 inch, 6 × 10.5 cm AA, 8 × 53 cm torpedo tubes. Shown as at Montevideo in December 1939 with false bow wave painted on and disruptive painting on superstructure.

47. Alisma, Corvette, U.K., 1942.
925 tons, 16 knots, 205 × 33 × 11½ ft, 1 × 4 inch, 1 × 2 pdr.
Early 'Flower' class with short forecastle and original mast and bridge layout. Painted in Western Approaches scheme.

48. Surprise, Corvette, U.S.A., 1944.
925 tons, 16 knots, 205 × 33 × 14½ ft, 2 × 3 inch.
'Flower' class with later type modifications, including long forecastle and revised bridge and mast layout. Canadian-built ship (ex H.M.S. *Heliotrope*) supplied to U.S. Navy. Measure 16 camouflage.

49. West Point, Troopship, U.S.A., 1945.
23,179 tons (gross), 22 knots, 723 × 93½ ×
32¼ ft.
Ex-U.S.S. *America* of United States Lines,
converted to troopship, 1941. Shown in
Measure 33 camouflage. *Inset.* U.S. Navy
patrol blimp.

50. Rockingham, Destroyer, U.K., 1943.

1,090 tons, 35 knots, $314\frac{1}{2} \times 31\frac{3}{4} \times 8\frac{3}{4}$ ft, 1×4 inch, 1×3 inch, 5×20 mm, one set of torpedo tubes.

'Town' class destroyer, ex-U.S. Navy flush-decker, one of 50 supplied to Britain. Modified with cut-down funnels and Type 271 radar for escort work. Shown in Western Approaches colour scheme.

51. Reuben James, Destroyer, U.S.A., 1941.

1,190 tons, 35 knots, $314\frac{1}{2} \times 31\frac{3}{4} \times 8\frac{3}{4}$ ft, 4×4 inch, 1×3 inch, 12×21 inch torpedo tubes.

Standard U.S. Navy flush-deck destroyer built 1919, in original condition. First U.S. warship sunk by U-boat in October 1941. Measure 2 camouflage.

52. Long Island, Escort Carrier, U.S.A., 1944.
11,300 tons, 18 knots, 492 × 69½ × 25½ ft, 1 × 5 inch, 2 × 3 inch.
Prototype escort carrier, converted 1941. Shown in Measure 32 camouflage in 1944.
Carried about 20 aircraft.

53. Ameer, Escort Carrier, U.K., 1943.
11,420 tons, 17 knots, 492 × 69½ × 25½ ft, 2 × 4 inch, 16 × 40 mm, 20 × 20 mm.
Standard conversion from merchant hull, 'Ruler' class, built in U.S.A. In camouflage scheme applied in U.S.A. to Admiralty requirements. Carried 18/24 aircraft.

54. Howe, Battleship, U.K., 1944.
35,000 tons, 28½ knots, 745 × 103 × 34 ft,
10 × 14 inch, 16 × 5.25 inch, 48 × 2 pdr,
1 × 40 mm, 7 × 20 mm.
Shown in Admiralty Intermediate Disruptive camouflage scheme.

55. PT.139, MTB, U.S.A., 1942.
38 tons, 40 knots, 80 × 20¾ × 5 ft, 2 × 20 mm, 4 × 21 inch torpedo tubes.
'Elco'-type PT boat in local camouflage scheme.

56. PT-77, MTB, U.S.A., 1942.
35 tons, 41 knots, 78×20¼×5¼ ft, 1×40 mm,
2×20 mm, 4×21 inch torpedo tubes.
'Higgins'-type PT boat as first built. This boat was
subsequently lost in action. Measure 2 type colour
scheme.

57. Richard Beitzen, Destroyer, Germany, 1940.
2,200 tons, 38 knots, 374 × 37 ft, 5 × 5 inch, 4 × 37 mm.
'Leberecht Maass' class destroyer in 1939-40 colour scheme.

58. Franklin, Aircraft Carrier, U.S.A., 1945.
27,100 tons, 33 knots, 872 × 93 × 28¼ ft, 12 × 5 inch, 44 × 40 mm. 'Essex' class short-hull attack carrier. Severely damaged by enemy air attack, February 1945. Measure 14 camouflage as in February 1945. *Inset.* Hellcat fighter showing tail marking for *Franklin's* air group, 1945.

59. Hornet (II), Aircraft Carrier, U.S.A., 1945.

27,100 tons, 33 knots, 872 × 93 × 28¼ ft, 12 × 5 inch, 44 × 40 mm. 'Essex' class short-hull attack carrier. This ship originally *Kearsage* was renamed in honour of the first *Hornet*. Measure 32 camouflage. *Inset*. Helldiver of *Hornet's* air group in 1945.

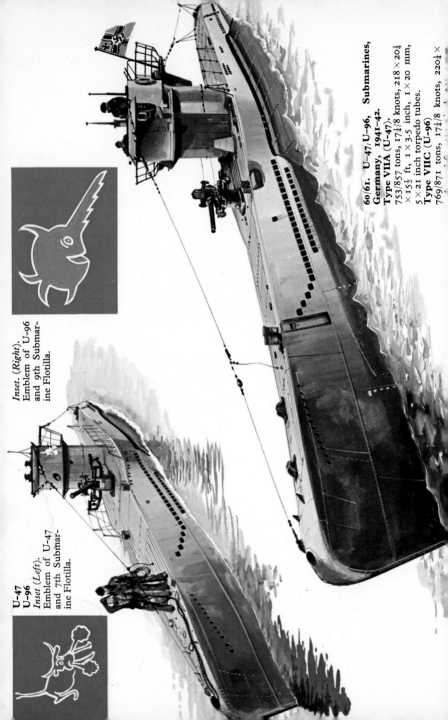

U-47
U-96

Inset (Left). Emblem of U-47 and 7th Submarine Flotilla.

Inset. (Right). Emblem of U-96 and 9th Submarine Flotilla.

60/61. U-47, U-96, Submarines, Germany, 1941–42.
Type VIIA (U-47).
753/857 tons, 17¼/8 knots, 218 × 20¼ × 15½ ft, 1 × 3.5 inch, 1 × 20 mm, 5 × 21 inch torpedo tubes.
Type VIIC (U-96)
769/871 tons, 17¼/8 knots, 220¼ ×

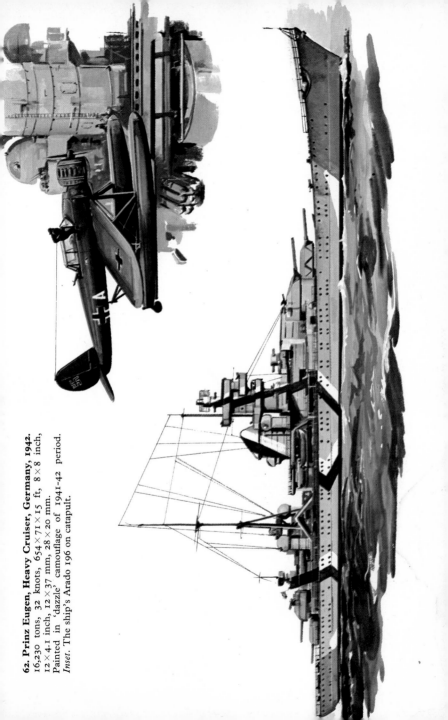

62. Prinz Eugen, Heavy Cruiser, Germany, 1942.
16,230 tons, 32 knots, 654 × 71 × 15 ft, 8 × 8 inch,
12 × 4.1 inch, 12 × 37 mm, 28 × 20 mm.
Painted in 'dazzle' camouflage of 1941-42 period.
Inset. The ship's Arado 196 on catapult.

63. Arkansas, Battleship, U.S.A., 1944.
26,100 tons, 21 knots, 562 × 106¼ × 26 ft, 12 × 12 inch, 6 × 5 inch, 10 × 3 inch, 36 × 40 mm.
Oldest battleship in service in U.S. Navy in World War 2 (built 1910-12) much modified. Measure 22 camouflage at time of Normandy landings.

64. Augusta, Heavy Cruiser, U.S.A., 1941.
9,050 tons, 32½ knots, 600¼ × 66½ × 16¼ ft, 9 × 8 inch, 8 × 5 inch, 32 × 40 mm, 27 × 20 mm. 'Northampton' class cruiser built 1930-32. Early application of Measure 22 camouflage, as flagship of Comtaskforce 1 in August 1941.

65. Hood, Battle-cruiser, U.K., 1941.
42,100 tons, 31 knots, 860½ × 105 × 28½ ft, 8 × 15 inch,
14 × 4 inch, 24 × 2 pdr.
Shown as at the *Bismarck* action, May 1941.

66. Exeter, Heavy Cruiser, U.K., 1939.
8,400 tons, 32 knots, 575 × 58 × 20 ft, 6 × 8 inch, 4 × 4 inch, 2 × 2 pdr. Shown as at Battle of River Plate, December 1939. *Inset.* Ship's badge.

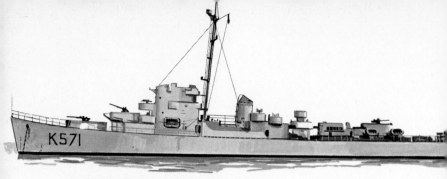

67. Inman, Destroyer Escort, U.K., 1943.
1,085 tons, 21 knots, $289\frac{1}{2} \times 35 \times 8\frac{1}{4}$ ft, 3×3 inch, 4×40 mm, $4/5 \times 20$ mm.
U.S.-built, short-hull DE.

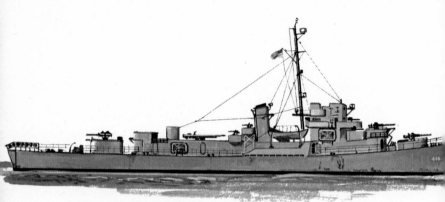

68. England, Destroyer Escort, U.S.A., 1943.
1,400 tons, 28 knots, $306 \times 37 \times 9\frac{1}{2}$ ft, 3×3 inch, 6×40 mm.
DE (long hull). Measure 14 camouflage.

69. Robert F. Keller, Destroyer Escort, U.S.A., 1946.
1,350 tons, 21 knots, $306 \times 37 \times 9$ ft, 2×5 inch, 10×40 mm.
'John C. Butler' class. Measure 13 camouflage, 1946.

70. Nicholas, Destroyer, U.S.A., 1942.
2,050 tons, 36 knots, $376\frac{1}{4} \times 39\frac{1}{2} \times 17\frac{3}{4}$ ft, 5×5 inch, 10×40 mm, 20×20 mm. Early 'Fletcher' class, shown in Measure 12 camouflage scheme, 1942.

71. **Nashville, Cruiser, U.S.A., 1943.**
9,745 tons, 34 knots, 608½ × 61¼ × 19¼ ft,
15 × 6 inch, 8 × 5 inch, 28 × 40 mm,
24 × 20 mm.
'Brooklyn' class light cruiser in Measure 33
camouflage.

1. **Patrick Henry:** Liberty Ship, U.S.A.

During World War 1 there was a massive merchant shipbuilding programme in the U.S.A., but although this was completed too late to assist the war effort, it was to satisfy most of America's commercial cargo shipping requirements in the following decade. By 1936, however, it was realised that the American merchant fleet was both ageing and operating at a commercial disadvantage compared with other big maritime powers. There was no provision for rapid expansion of the fleet in the event of war and little incentive for operators to build new ships. This led to the setting up of the United States Maritime Commission to administer subsidies, organise new building facilities and supervise merchant ship operating patterns. In 1937 the U.S.M.C. instituted a ten-year programme aiming to produce fifty new ships a year, and providing the modernised yard facilities to achieve this. Various standard cargo ships were designed, suitable for different trade routes. A good deal of long-term planning was done to allow for greatly increased output of ships should the need arise, and some initial ideas were worked

out for the incorporation of large-scale prefabrication and other industrial methods into what was still largely a 'traditional' shipbuilding industry, even in the United States.

By early 1939, when war seemed inevitable, the ten-year programme was doubled to 100 ships a year, and a year later, after the fall of France, it was again doubled to 200 ships a year. In the meantime the first of the U.S.M.C. standard ships had entered service successfully and met with approval; one of them was the first American merchant ship to be of welded construction throughout. The standard ships showed that the initial U.S.M.C. ideas were on the right lines, but the ships were, if anything, too elaborate to be built quickly in the even bigger numbers which would be required, and with a relative shortage of manpower and yards in which to build them.

Britain in this 1940 period was hard-pressed and the German U-Boats were already taking a huge toll of British merchant shipping – well over 1 million tons were sunk in the first year of the war and British yards needed not only to replace sunken tonnage but also to expand the fleet. It was proving an impossible task, and an official Merchant

Shipbuilding Mission was sent to the U.S.A. in a quest to order ships from American yards. Leader of the British mission was from the shipbuilding firm of J. L. Thompson and Sons of Sunderland. Plans adapted from a 1939 design were taken of a dry cargo steamer, *Donington Court*. One particular virtue of the design was that only a small engine could give its 10,000 tons a sea speed of 11 knots. Britain wanted sixty of these ships built in the U.S.A. and the two contracts, for thirty each, to be known as the 'Ocean' class were placed with Todd Shipyards and the Henry S. Kaiser firm. The U.S.M.C. was not impressed with the idea of these slow, simple, 11 knot ships which compared unfavourably with the fast turbine drive (17 knots) of the new U.S.M.C. standard type.

However, by early 1941 it became apparent to the U.S. Maritime Commission, that the yards would not be able to meet their now increasing requirement for new tonnage. There was a particular shortage of turbine machinery. One answer was to look afresh at the British 'Ocean' class design and adapt it ruthlessly to cut out all frills and suit it for mass-production on a grand scale. Among changes made were the merging of the original 'twin islands' into a single 'island' superstructure, shifting all the crew accommodation and services (bathrooms, galley, etc.) into this structure, eliminating deck camber and all unnecessary curved plating, reducing woodwork to bare essentials, and making other changes, such as providing steel bulwarks instead of guardrails, to cut down on materials and building time. Topmasts were not provided and the early ships lacked radio direction finders, gyro compasses, emergency generators, and other facilities, though some or all of these desirable fittings were included in later units. Steam reciprocating engines of 2,500 indicated horsepower, and water-tube boilers were specified, these being based on the British design. All parts were rigidly standardised so that engine fittings, for instance, could be sent to any yard or any ship.

The design was quickly finalised and the first of many ships of the new type was laid down. The new programme was announced in February 1941, and nine shipyards were authorised that year for new construction work. At first the austere, and functional-looking ship earned such nicknames as 'Ugly Duckling', but clearly something more suited and 'official' was needed. The president of the U.S.M.C. thought of the name 'Liberty Ship' and the very appropriate name *Patrick Henry* was chosen for the first ship. Thereafter most Liberty ships were named after American patriots or distinguished citizens. The *Patrick Henry* was built in 150 days on the slip and launched on 27 September 1941 – called 'Liberty Ship Day'. Another 95 days were taken in fitting out.

Fast as this was, the ever increasing speed of production became legendary and has not been surpassed since. Among the many yards which came into Liberty ship construction, speed of production sometimes became an unofficial competition. Ships were produced in 10 days, and the fastest of all was *Robert E. Peary*, built in 4 days 15 hours. Mass-production on a scale unprecedented in shipbuilding made this sort of achievement possible, components being built inland and delivered to the site. In the new yards, conventional slipways and stocks were dispensed with, and ships were 'assembled' in a basin or dry dock. Welding was the common means of fast assembly though some yards retained riveting.

The welding led to some fracturing and, in extreme cases some ships split in two; subsequent measures to prevent this included strengthening hatchways and other parts, and new methods of battening. The relatively few instances of loss or severe damage due to poor welding and stresses gave Liberty ships a bad reputation in some uninformed quarters. But when it is remembered that over 2,700 vessels were built, the rate of structural failure was very small. In actual fact the Liberty ships were extremely tough, and the well compartmented design enabled them to withstand a fair amount of battle damage on occasion. Many survived torpedo hits or gunfire even though severely damaged and flooded by any usual standard.

While Liberty ships were not the only 'war standard' cargo ships built, they were the most numerous of all, and in their undramatic way they were as important to the Allies as all their fleets of warships. For the Liberty ships were the carriers of the war material and merchandise which enabled the Allied nations to wage war. The Liberty ships crossed every ocean, in nearly every convoy, in all weathers and conditions. About

200 were supplied to the British merchant marine and fifty to the Soviet Union as Lend-Lease material. The original Liberty ship scheme envisaged a life of five years – in fact an expendable ship – but some steamed on for as long as thirty years after 1945, under all flags. During World War 2 Liberty ships were adapted for many duties – colliers, tankers, landing ships, troopships, stores ships, depot ships, and hospital ships. Nine Liberty ships were sunk as breakwaters on the Normandy coast in June 1944. One ship, *Stephen Hopkins*, had the distinction of sinking a German armed raider, the *Stier*, in a 1942 gun duel in the South Atlantic – and was herself sunk in the same action. *Patrick Henry* was completed while America was still neutral, so had no guns initially, but once U.S.A. entered the war, armament became standard – a 4 inch gun on 'bandstands' fore and aft, plus 20 mm Oerlikons or machine guns on the island superstructure was typical armament. *Patrick Henry* is shown as built in the standard overall dark shade known as 'Ocean Gray' which was applied to Maritime Commission ships at that time. *Patrick Henry* survived the war with an unremarkable career,

though her first voyage took her to Egypt with military supplies and she was the first American ship to pass through the Suez Canal after America declared war.

2. **Ocean Liberty:** Ocean/PF Ship, U.S.A./U.K.

While the Liberty ship became the most numerous and important of Allied war emergency cargo ships, the design from which the Liberty ship evolved was wholly British in the first instance. The British requirements were initially to replace tonnage lost in the early months of the war and the British Merchant Shipbuilding Mission of September 1940 took a set of plans with them to U.S.A. as related above. Had the United States not been dragged so close to a war footing (even before her official involvement in hostilities), the Liberty ship might not have come about. *Ocean Liberty* represents the British idea of what was required and the British mission ordered sixty of this 'Ocean' class in U.S.A. as previously described, the design being a simplified adaptation of J. L. Thompson Ltd's 1939 tramp steamer of which the first had been *Donington Court. Ocean Liberty* was laid down in Kaiser's Todd-Bath Yard, Portland, Maine, in May 1941 as the first of thirty ships, and a sister vessel *Ocean Vanguard* was laid down down in Kaiser's Todd-California Yard, Richmond, California, in April 1941 as the first of the thirty ships built at this yard. All the ships were completed by the end of 1942, but no more of this type were ordered since by then the full Liberty ship programme was under way. The early 'Ocean' class ships, however, were the first of the war emergency cargo types in service. The twin island superstructure was a feature eliminated on the later Liberty ships, as were the guardrails. Dimensions were similar. Length overall: 425 ft. Beam: 57 ft. Reciprocating engine of 2,500 ihp, and speed 11 knots, 7,174 tons gross. A distinctive feature of the 'Oceans' was that they were coal-fired, since coal was readily available in Britain and oil supplies were considered less certain in Britain in the 1940 period. They may well have been the last big coal-fired ships built in the U.S.A. The reciprocating engines were of British design, but built in the U.S.A. by General Machinery Co., Hamilton, Ohio,

and the same engines were subsequently used for the entire Liberty ship programme.

While the 'Oceans' were being built in the U.S.A., about seventy vessels of generally similar design were built in British yards. These were known in Britain as the PF (pre-fabricated) class, the first being *Empire Liberty* built by Thompsons of Sunderland in 1941. Thompson built a number of these ships identical to the 'Oceans' – since they originated the design – but ships built in other British yards differed in various points of detail and dimensions according to the facilities and traditions of the builders. It is interesting to note that while the Liberty design as finally evolved merged all the upperworks into a single island for simplicity of construction, the British Ministry of War Transport which sanctioned the PF design favoured the split-island layout since it ensured that sub-assemblies for bridge, funnel, boat deck, etc., could be handled by the smaller capacity cranes in many British yards. The PF ships were pre-fabricated to a degree, though never on the great industrialised scale of the Liberty ships. *Ocean Liberty* is representative of all these early war emergency ships and is shown as she appeared in 1942. She was still sailing (under another name) in the 1960s.

3. **Fort Wallace:** North Sands Ship, Canada/U.K.

As well as contracting with United States yards for the 'Ocean' class of freighters, the British Merchant Shipbuilding Mission also contracted with some Canadian yards for ships of a similar type. Some twenty-six ships were ordered, the first being laid down in April 1941. Again the design of *Donington Court* was used as a pattern. While the 'Oceans' were all-welded, however, the Canadian-built version (known as the 'North Sands' type) were largely riveted in construction, for Canadian yards were poorly equipped by comparison with U.S. yards. In fact, the Canadian achievement in building war emergency freighters was quite considerable, for Canadian yards were small and few, and a shipbuilding industry had to build up from scratch with even less of an existing framework than the U.S. shipbuilding industry enjoyed. The 'North Sands' type ship – all named after Forts – were much increased in output from the ori-

ginal twenty-six – well over 100 more were built, some under Lend-Lease terms ordered by the United States.

In the meantime the Canadian Maritime Commission had worked out an improved version of the basic design in the light of experience. The new type, known as the 'Victory' class, was similar to the 'North Sands' but changes included different hatches, and a longer shelter deck with the lifeboats grouped together, and water-tube boilers replacing the Scotch type boilers previously used. The big change was that oil fuel replaced coal. Depending on the builder, 'Victory' ships had more welding in their construction than the previous ships. The 'Victory' ships went into production in 1943. They were $441\frac{1}{2}$ ft in overall length, 57 ft beam, and were 7,150 tons gross. The speed was 11 knots. Most of the 'Victory' ships were armed as built, with a single 4 inch gun fore and aft, and 20 mm Oerlikon guns in the bridge wings. These ships proved tough and durable, some of them surviving into the 1960s and even the 1970s. A number were taken into Royal Canadian Navy and Royal Navy service on completion for use as fleet stores ships, repair ships, and depot ships and most remained in service in these roles for many years post-war.

The vessel shown, *Fort Wallace*, is typical of the whole class though there were detail variations in the number of derricks. The wood frame at the bow on this particular ship supported an external degaussing cable which carried an electric current to neutralise the ship's magnetism as a measure to combat the threat of magnetic mines. The ship is painted in the standard 1943–45 period finish for merchant ships laid down for new construction by the Canadian Maritime Commission – a light sea grey with white masts and structures above bridge level (funnel excepted). This scheme was found to give a good compromise in low visibility in North Atlantic waters, the white areas tending to 'merge' into the sky background when the ship was hull down. The 'Victory' ships were succeeded by a similar design, the 'Canadian' class, which had the option of oil or coal bunkerage, and other detail changes, including a reversion to the original 'North Sands' class disposition of lifeboats. Most later 'Victory' and 'Canadian' ships had additional light AA armament. Well over 450 cargo ships were built by Canadian yards in World War 2, making a big contribution to the Allied war effort. Unlike the American 'Liberty' ships the Canadian 'Victory' ships were not mass-produced; for the most part they were built in traditional yards.

4. **Kirov**: Cruiser, U.S.S.R.

During the inter-war period, naval equipment in the Soviet Union received the lowest priority of all among the Russian armed forces. This was largely due to the most urgent need to devote the main defence resources to building up a strong army and air force. In addition the sea frontiers of the U.S.S.R. were relatively small and widely divided, and the Bolsheviks inherited only a few remnants of the once great fleet of Imperial Russia – most of it was destroyed or badly damaged in the operations against the White Russians and the Allies in 1917–22. Very little was done by the Soviets in the way of naval activity until the early 1930s, save the refitting of what ships were salved from the earlier fighting and the establishment of a properly organised and trained naval service, and some naval ports.

However, some resources for naval re-equipment – more generous than ever before – were allocated in the Second Five Year Plan of 1934. To build up the surface fleet some powerful new cruisers able to act as commerce raiders were considered most important, and the Italian 'Condottieri' class, then the most modern design, was chosen as a basis for a very similar design for the Soviet Navy, and the Italian firm of Ansaldo, Genoa, builders of the 'Condottieri' class, made plans for an enlarged version available to the Russians. This resulted in the very handsome 'Kirov' class, the name ship being laid down in Putilov, Leningrad, dockyard in 1934 and launched in December 1936. *Kirov* herself was followed by *Maxim Gorki*, a year behind in the same yard and these were the only two of the class actually commissioned (in 1938 and 1940 respectively) before the Soviet Union became involved in the war. Two other ships, *Molotov* and *Voroshilov* were built at Nicholayev in the Black Sea and did not complete until late in the war, while two others, *Kalinin* and *Kaganovitch* were not completed until after the war.

Italian ideas accorded with Soviet requirements for short sea operations, most important being high speed and good armament, so armour protection and range were sacrificed to this end. Diesel engines were fitted for cruising (giving the respectable speed of 17 knots) in addition to the conventional turbines and boilers. Each engine was grouped with its own boilers and auxiliaries to minimise the chances of the ship being immobilised completely by damage – each power arrangement was independent of the other. Shaft horsepower of 110,000 gave 35 knots – a very high speed for a ship of its size. The main armament of nine 7·1 inch guns was arranged in three triple turrets, with six 3·9 inch AA guns in single mountings (three each side abreast of the after funnel) and six 13 mm AA guns, three each side abreast the bridge. There were two triple 21 inch torpedo tubes and an aircraft and catapult were provided between the funnels. Up to ninety mines could be carried and dropped by twin chutes aft. The cruising range was 4,000 miles at 15 knots.

Kirov joined the Red Banner Baltic Fleet immediately on commissioning and as the most modern large unit of the fleet she saw much action in the war years, even though Soviet naval activities were confined to relatively small-scale operations. The first action for *Kirov* was to lead a bombardment against Finnish forts at Hango in December 1939 during the Soviet blockade of Finnish ports in the Russo-Finnish war. *Kirov* sustained some shell damage herself in this action. When the German fleet moved up the Baltic in June 1941, supporting the invasion of Russia, *Kirov* was again in action. Her sister *Maxim Gorki* was mined early on, leaving *Kirov* as the only big cruiser in the fleet. The German Army moved rapidly up the Baltic coast taking the seaports but by August 1941 *Kirov* was taking a major part in providing gunfire support for the Red Army in holding the important port of Revel. When the Germans finally closed in on the port, *Kirov* led the evacuation of all the small naval and merchant ships in the port, providing covering fire against both shore and air targets. The Germans were now masters of the Baltic, bottling up the surviving units of the Red Banner Fleet in the Gulf of Finland where operations centred on Leningrad and Kronstadt with large units confined only to some bombardment work and AA defence until the tide of war turned west in the 1944–45

period. The Soviets fought a very cautious war in the Baltic with most of the action being of a coastal nature and involving small craft. There were no major fleet actions involving large surface vessels – so *Kirov* never had to engage a German cruiser. In post-war years, *Kirov* served on, with slight modernisation, and was still in the active fleet as a training cruiser in the 1970s, a remarkably young-looking veteran of World War 2 and one of the oldest cruisers still afloat.

Details: displacement – 8,800 tons (standard), 11,500 tons (full load); length 626 ft overall; beam 59 ft; draught 17 ft; armour plate 3 inch (side), 2 inch deck, 4 inch on turrets; complement 734 officers and men.

Kirov is shown in the Baltic colour scheme of 1944–45.

5. Oktyabrskaya Revolutsia: Battleship, U.S.S.R.

This quite distinctive and ungainly old battleship was one of a class of four, built for the old Imperial Russian Navy in the 1909–15 period, to a basic Italian design. The unusual feature is the canting back of the fore funnel to keep smoke clear of the range-finding equipment in the control top. By any standards the ships of this class were obsolete by 1940 and one, the *Poltava*, had been scrapped in 1923 after damage in the 1917–22 Revolutionary War.

Oktyabrskaya Revolutsia displaced 23,606 tons (26,000 tons full load), was 619 ft long, had a 87 ft beam and a draught of $27\frac{1}{2}$ ft. She followed the original 'Dreadnought' style of armament disposition, four triple 12 inch turrets disposed at one level, without super-firing, and had a side battery of twelve 4·7 inch guns in casemates firing on the broadside. Some small AA machine guns were augmented during World War 2 by eight 3 inch and twelve 37 mm AA guns. There was a 9 inch armour belt and 3 inches of deck armour. Complement was 1,200 men. The original top speed was 23 knots, achieved by 50,000 shp. There were twenty-five boilers. She was launched in October 1911 and commissioned early in 1914.

By 1939 she was a somewhat run-down vessel, much slower than her designed speed and offering a low standard of accommodation. She and her sisters were really fit only for scrapping and some naval historians believe they were largely retained because Stalin – not a naval man –

considered battleships of any condition to have some sort of prestige value at the time.

Because they were available at the outbreak of war, however, the three surviving ships saw quite hard service. On 18 December 1939, *Oktyabrskaya Revolutsia* brought her guns to bear on the Finnish port of Koivisto. Her sister ship *Marat* and a destroyer flotilla were also involved, in what proved to be a brisk bombardment, *Marat* suffering some damage in the return fire. In the 1941–42 period the ship was mainly engaged in defensive work in the Gulf of Finland. In a German air raid on Kronstadt, *Marat* was sunk and her stern remains to this day, preserved as a memorial to Soviet sailors killed in the defence of Kronstadt.

Oktyabrskaya Revolutsia played an important part in the siege of Leningrad, bombarding German troops, and she was subsequently involved in Russian re-entry into the Baltic. Her sister ship, *Sevastopol* (ex-*Pariskaya Kommuna*), was meanwhile acting as flagship for the Black Sea Fleet and gave particularly good service in the siege of Sevastopol, covering the smaller ships bringing in supplies for the defenders. It was because of this that she was renamed. Both *Sevastopol* and *Oktyabrskaya Revolutsia* remained on the Soviet fleet list until about 1960 before being officially stricken.

6. **Leningrad**: Destroyer, U.S.S.R.

The Soviet Second Five Year Plan of 1934 allowed for some new destroyers to complement the 'Kirov' class cruisers, and the result was the 'Leningrad' class in which inspiration was found from the big French 'Fantasque' class of *Contre-torpilleurs*. By previous standards destroyers of this size, well over 2,000 tons, were like light cruisers. French naval architects are believed to have been engaged to design the 'Leningrad' class vessels, and the resulting ship was handsome and purposeful in appearance, like a miniature 'Kirov'. The 'Leningrads' displaced 2,225 tons standard (2,580 tons full load), were 418½ ft in overall length, 38½ ft in beam, and of 13 ft draught. Three shaft geared turbines gave 70,000 shp and a top speed of 36–38 knots, though *Leningrad* achieved over 39 knots on trials. The three boiler rooms and engine rooms were grouped in independent units. There were six (later eight) 21 inch torpedo tubes in two mounts. The war armament was five 5·1 inch guns in single mounts, two forward, two aft, and one placed between the bridge and forefunnel. There were four 37 mm AA guns, two aft of the after funnel and one each side of the fore funnel. The main guns had limited elevation and the anti-aircraft capability of these ships was therefore restricted. Directors for the main armament were sited fore and aft, however, in cruiser fashion. The Russians classed these ships as *lideri* (leaders) and they were no doubt intended to act as flotilla leaders for a subsequent class of smaller destroyers which was also being built. Twelve 'Leningrad' class ships were laid down but work on at least three was suspended for the duration of hostilities and these were finished post-war.

Those ships completed between 1937 and 1940 saw quite arduous service, and *Kharkov* had an excellent record as one of the major (and most modern) units of the Black Sea Fleet. She was one of the ships which escorted the convoy of stores and troops which successfully relieved Odessa in October 1941. Previously in June 1941 she was in a small cruiser and destroyer squadron which bombarded the port of Constanta in an attempt to delay the German advance, and in this engagement her sister ship *Moskva* was sunk by mines. From August 1941 *Kharkov* was involved in the operations to relieve Sevastopol, bringing in supplies and giving gunfire support in the amphibious landings which were made in an attempt to break the siege. Gunfire support was the main task of the big ships in the Black Sea for the Germans only used small craft in this theatre. It was in a major bombardment of Yalta on the night of 5/6 October 1943, that *Kharkov* met her end. With two smaller destroyers she lingered too long near the shore and at first light was still within range of German land-based aircraft which promptly sank all three ships. After this blow to the surface fleet, in fact, the Russians tended to keep their larger ships safely in port, being unwilling to risk further losses on this scale.

7.   **AM.142:**   Minesweeper, U.S.A./U.S.S.R.

The naval war between Germany and Soviet Russia was characterised by mining on a consider-able scale. The Baltic and Arctic Sea theatres in particular saw huge minefields being laid by both sides. Among the most active Soviet ships, in fact, were minesweepers and minelayers of which the Soviet Navy had fairly ample numbers, albeit of the small coastal type. The Germans were able to master the simple Russian mines, but the technical sophistication of German mines proved much harder for the Soviets to tackle. When the United States started the Lease-Lend scheme the Soviet Navy made a particular request for minesweepers of the most modern type, able to deal with German acoustic and magnetic mines. Starting in August 1943 the U.S. Navy transferred ten brand new 'Admirable' class minesweepers to the Soviet Navy direct from the shipbuilders (Tampa Shipbuilding Co.), the first vessels of a new type designed for large scale production.

AM.142, originally U.S.S. *Apex*, was one of this first batch. These ships were 184½ ft in overall length, 33 ft beam, and 10 ft draught. Displacing 650 tons, they were powered by 1,710 shp diesel motors which gave a top speed of 14·5 knots. Complement was about one hundred men.

Lack of a conventional smoke stack was a distinctive feature though ships built later had a small funnel. Two 3 inch guns and four 20 mm Oerlikon guns constituted the armament, and 'O', 'LL', and acoustic sweep gear was carried. The ships were sailed to Greenock, Scotland, by U.S.N. crews then transferred to Soviet Navy crews who sailed them to Murmansk in November 1943 as part of the escort for a Russian convoy. Over 100 ships of this class were also completed for the U.S. Navy, and more than 100 others were completed as submarine chasers, with depth charge throwers replacing the sweep gear. The original U.S. Navy camouflage scheme was retained on the Russian vessels, as were the hull numbers. These ships served with the Northern Fleet.

When the war in Europe ended in May 1945, another twenty-four 'Admirable' class minesweepers were made available to the Soviet Navy but these went straight to the Pacific Fleet for operations which the Soviet Navy was planning against Japan. They all saw extensive inshore service in the various landings made in Korea. By the standards of Allied landings elsewhere, these Russian amphibious operations were on a small scale, the minesweepers sometimes being the largest supporting craft. Post-war all the surviving ships continued in Soviet Navy service for some years, though strictly speaking they should have been returned to the U.S.A. when hostilities ceased.

8. **Shtshuka class:** Submarine, U.S.S.R.

When the Soviet Navy was being built up, great priority was given to the establishment of a submarine fleet, so much so that with over 150 boats in 1939, Russia had the biggest underwater force in the world. By early 1940 this had increased to 175. Despite the enormous effort put into the submarine programme, the potential was never fully realised and the submarine service had a disappointing record. Only about 100 German merchant ships and about thirty small warships were sunk by Soviet submarines throughout the whole war period, even though official Soviet war histories make much more substantial claims. The poor results of Soviet submarine operations probably stemmed from the relatively short period in which it was built up in the few years preceding the outbreak of war. For there was no time to build up a tradition of fully experienced personnel. When war came, the submarines often patrolled in unfamiliar areas, most frequently in the shallow waters of the coastal shelf and in poor murky weather. A rigid operational pattern was imposed, which restricted individual boats to defined areas. Though the men were the pick of the service and proved excellent, there was little chance within the system for individual initiative and there were no tactical doctrines adopted, such as the 'Wolf Pack' systems used so successfully by the Germans and Americans.

The first submarine class built in some numbers (twenty-five) was the 'L' or 'Leninetz' class, based on the British 'L' class design of late World War I. One of the British boats, *L55*, sank near Kronstadt in 1919 and was salvaged in 1928. The 'L' class was built in the First Five Year Plan period from 1929. With the Second Five Year Plan came several different classes of which the medium size was the 'Sh' or 'Shtshuka' (Pike) class, of which an early example is illustrated. Over 100 of these were built in

the 1935–47 period. This type displaced 620 tons on the surface and 738 tons submerged. It was 190 ft long, 19½ ft beam, and drew 13 ft. Diesel motors gave a top surface speed of 15½ knots and batteries gave an underwater speed of 8½ knots. There were six 21 inch torpedo tubes forward. Early examples had a single 45 mm AA gun forward of the conning tower while later ones had a second gun abaft the tower. There were numerous detail differences between batches, though the long conning tower was fairly distinctive.

These 'Sh' boats took their name from the first vessel built. The largest of the new submarines was the 'K' class. This was a fine design with a particularly fast diving time. Of 1,457/2,062 tons, and 320 ft long, they could carry twelve torpedoes and thirty-two mines. The outbreak of war cut short the building programme. The 'K' boats made some mining sorties into Norwegian waters, and one, *K-21*, came very close to world fame in July 1942 when she penetrated the screen around the German battleship *Tirpitz* and found the great ship ahead of her. However, a great opportunity was missed when the boat's torpedoes failed to fire.

9. **Maluitka class:** Submarine, U.S.S.R.

The smallest of the three prewar standard classes was the 'M' or 'Maluitka' class, a coastal type of what was then a novel design. Because Russian shipyards were still restricted in capacity, the 'M' class were completely pre-fabricated, built inland in sections at various engineering plants, mostly at Gorki, and assembled on any suitable slipway. The thinking behind this was to have a class of submarine which could be built quickly and in great numbers in time of war. In the event nearly 300 were eventually built, but tanks and aircraft took priority once war was declared.

The early 'M' class, *M1–M99*, had small low conning towers and displaced 161 tons, or 202 tons underwater. Only 124 ft long and 10 ft in beam, they had a single 45 mm AA gun on the forward casing. Surface and submerged speeds were 13 and 7 knots respectively. The later *M-100* onwards, had a higher sided conning tower with a windshield and is the type illustrated. These were longer boats at 146 ft with a displacement of 205/256 tons. There was a crew of only twenty. Being of a handy size

they mostly stayed in coastal waters. On a number of occasions they were used to land saboteurs or re-supply partisans behind enemy lines. The 'M' class were mostly built in the 1935–41 period and represented a large proportion of the Soviet underseas fleet on the outbreak of war. Because of their small size and pre-fabricated nature, a number were taken by rail on the Trans-Siberian railway and assembled in Vladivostock to re-inforce the Soviet Pacific Fleet.

10. **Georges Leygues:** Light Cruiser, France

The six cruisers of the 'La Galissonnière' class were among the most modern of French warships in commission at the outbreak of war. They were designed to keep within the Washington Treaty limitations and proved to have a happy combination of size, speed, and armament which made them most useful warships. The first two ships of the class *La Galissonnière* and *Jean de Vienne* were ordered under the 1931 estimates, and the remaining four, *Gloire*, *Marseillaise*, *Montcalm*, and *Georges Leygues*, were built under the 1932 estimates. All were commissioned by the end of 1937. The displacement was 7,600 tons standard, and 9,120 tons at full load. They were 581 ft long, 57½ ft in beam, and 17½ ft in draught. The geared turbines gave 84,000 shp, on two shafts, with a designed speed of 31 knots. However, all exceeded 35 knots on trials, and sometimes did so in service. They had a range of 5,440 miles at 15 knots. The original armament was nine 6 inch guns in three triple turrets, eight 3.5 inch AA guns, and eight 13.2 mm AA guns, plus four 21.7 inch torpedo tubes. An aircraft catapult was carried on the after 6 inch turret and a single Loire 130 flying boat was attached to each ship.

After the fall of France, *Gloire*, *Montcalm*, and *Georges Leygues* were sent from their port of internment, Toulon, in September 1940 to sail for Dakar which was under the control of the Vichy French. *Gloire* eventually went to Casablanca, but the other two vessels arrived at Dakar and stayed there for some time as part of the port's defences. The other three ships were all at Toulon where they were scuttled following the German occupation of the South of France in November 1942. Though two of them were later raised by the Italians, they were never again

effective ships, and were subsequently sunk by Allied bombing. Dakar went over to the Allied cause in late 1942 and *Montcalm*, *Georges Leygues*, and *Gloire* henceforth worked under Free French control. *Georges Leygues* made an early cruise which resulted in her sinking an armed German raiding vessel near the Equator. However, all three ships were in a state of neglect and mechanical deficiency due to the circumstances of the previous two years. They were therefore sent to Philadelphia Navy Yard for refit up to the best standards. The aircraft catapult was removed, radar was fitted, and six U.S. Navy pattern quad 40 mm AA mounts were fitted, plus sixteen Oerlikon 20 mm AA guns. The low silhouette and spacious decks of the ships gave these AA guns very good arcs of fire.

Subsequently all three surviving units of this class saw strenuous service with the Allies. *Georges Leygues*, together with *Montcalm*, formed part of the large Allied naval force which provided covering fire for the Normandy landings, these ships operating off Omaha beach. Later they formed the main part of a largely French naval task force which covered the Allied landings in the South of France at Provence, and were chosen to lead the naval forces covering the liberation of Corsica which was a wholly French operation.

The three ships continued to serve for many years post-war. *Georges Leygues* herself was built at the Penhoët yard, launched in March 1936 and completed in December 1937. The illustration shows her as in 1944 after the refit in America, with augmented AA armament and painted in the standard U.S. Navy finish of the time, MEASURE 22.

11. **Strasbourg:** Battleship, France

Pride of the French Navy in the immediate pre-war period were the two handsome battleships *Dunkerque* and *Strasbourg*, which had been laid down in December 1932 and November 1934 respectively, and completed in 1937 and 1938. *Dunkerque* represented the French Navy at the British Coronation Review in May 1937. Built to conform to the Washington Treaty limitations, the designers took some inspiration from the British *Nelson* and *Rodney*, grouping the main armament forward of the bridge in two quadruple 13 inch turrets. These

were quite widely spaced to separate the magazines. The secondary armament was sixteen 5·1 inch dual purpose guns in twin turrets, and there were eight 37 mm AA guns and thirty-two 13·2 mm AA guns. A catapult was located right aft, with a derrick for handling aircraft. Two Loire 130 flying boats could be carried. Conning tower and control tops were located in the main superstructure, with a secondary control top position aft. There were detail differences in the structures of the two ships. The displacement was 26,500 tons, 33,000 tons full load. Length was 702 ft overall, beam 101 ft. Four shaft geared turbines generated 1,000,000 shp, giving a designed speed of 29½ knots, though 31½ knots could be achieved. Armour protection was extensive with 355 mm of armour plate on the turrets and conning tower, 225 mm on the waterline armoured belt, 180 mm at main deck level, plus two armoured decks of 125 mm and 50 mm each. Built into the hull were two longitudinal torpedo bulkheads of 30 mm each in thickness. The crew numbered about 1,400 officers and men. *Dunkerque* was built in drydock in Brest naval yard – her bow being built as a separate section –

and *Strasbourg* was built by Penhoët yard, St. Nazaire.

Despite being well-known and prestigious ships, the course of events in World War 2 doomed them to a sorry end. *Dunkerque* and *Strasbourg* were at the North African base of Mers-el-Kebir when the French armistice with Germany was signed. The two battleships, among others, were to be disarmed. A British force under Admiral Sir James Somerville in *Hood*, gave the French ships an ultimatum either to join the British fleet, or to steam to either Britain or the West Indies under British control. The French naval command rejected the ultimatum, and the British force fired on the French ships. *Dunkerque* was hit and damaged, and three days later, on 6 July 1940, she was torpedoed by Swordfish aircraft from H.M.S. *Ark Royal*. Though later salved and towed to Toulon for refit, *Dunkerque* was subsequently scuttled when Toulon was occupied by the Germans in 1942. *Strasbourg* escaped to make for Toulon, but en route she was also attacked by Swordfish from *Ark Royal*. She was hit but not disabled. After repair she lay at Toulon until November 1942 when she was also scuttled. In due course she was raised and

repaired but was bombed and sunk by Allied aircraft in August 1944. The only shots fired in anger by the two ships were a few salvoes fired by *Dunkerque* at H.M.S. *Hood* in the Mers-el-Kebir engagement. *Strasbourg* had also made a short sally in late 1939 in the chase of the *Graf Spee*, but was too late to share the honours in its destruction.

The illustration shows *Strasbourg* as she appeared in 1940, carrying 'neutrality' markings (French national colours) on the second turret.

12.   **Richelieu:**   Battleship, France

A new slightly enlarged 'Richelieu' class was designed to follow *Dunkerque* and *Strasbourg*, and the first two, *Richelieu* and *Jean Bart* were allowed for in the 1935 naval estimates. *Richelieu* was laid down in October of that year. The ships were built to the full Washington Treaty limits, of 35,000 tons displacement standard and 47,500 tons full load. The length was $813\frac{1}{2}$ ft overall, $116\frac{1}{2}$ ft in beam, and draught was 30 ft. Two quadruple turrets, carrying eight 15 inch guns, were disposed forward and the entire design and layout was similar to *Strasbourg* except for the funnel arrangement which was incorporated in distinctive style into the after superstructure. The four shaft geared turbines gave a top speed of 30 knots (though 32 knots was achieved) from 179,000 shp. The main armour belt was 400 mm at the waterline and 225 mm at the main deck. There were three armoured decks with thicknesses of 130 mm, 170 mm, and 40 mm. The turrets had a maximum thickness of 430 mm, and the conning tower had main armour 340 mm thick. The designed secondary armament was nine 6 inch guns in three triple turrets aft, and twelve 4 inch guns. Fourteen twin 57 mm turrets would have formed the rest of the AA armament. However, the final armament was not fitted before *Richelieu* and *Jean Bart* had seen some eventful war service. *Richelieu* was actually built in dry dock at Brest Navy Yard, and was launched in January 1939. A later sister ship, the *Clemenceau*, was building in Brest when France was over-run, and she was bombed by the Allies and wrecked before completion. *Jean Bart* was built at St. Nazaire but escaped to Casablanca, still far from complete, when the Germans took France. She stayed at Casablanca throughout the war and was completed in the 1945–49 period.

Richelieu was almost complete in July 1940, and sailed from France to Dakar. The British gave an ultimatum to French ships at Dakar – join the British or be sunk – and after the French forces refused to accept the terms, the British attempted to blow up *Richelieu* by placing charges under the stern. These did not explode, so a torpedo attack was made by aircraft from H.M.S. *Hermes*. She was hit at the stern but rested in shallow water and remained as part of Dakar's defences until Dakar joined the Allied cause. In January 1943, now available to the Free French, she sailed for a refit in U.S.A. Here the AA armament was greatly augmented by U.S. Navy pattern quad 40 mm Bofors guns, sixty pieces in all, plus fifty 20 mm Oerlikons, and American fire control equipment and radar. The aircraft catapult and crane originally carried aft were removed in this refit. In November 1943, the refitted *Richelieu* joined the British Home Fleet. Then in March 1944 she sailed to join the British East Indies Fleet, via the Suez Canal. In July 1944 she took part in the bombardment of Sabang; she returned to Casablanca in October 1944 and returned to the East Indies Fleet in January 1945. More fire support actions took place against Japanese shore targets. When the war ended *Richelieu* moved on to Indo-China waters when France was still engaged in a guerrilla warfare campaign. When first refitted *Richelieu* was painted in U.S. Navy style, but the illustration shows her as in 1944–45, when she was painted in a version of the British Admiralty Light Standard Design to conform to the practice of the East Indies Fleet.

13. **Béarn:** Aircraft Carrier, France

Béarn was France's only aircraft carrier and she was originally intended to be a battleship of the 'Lorraine' class in World War I. However, the hull was kept incomplete and in 1920 work was resumed to convert her to aircraft carrier form. She eventually commissioned as a carrier in May 1927. She was 593 ft long, and 114 ft in beam. She had an 80 mm side armour belt and a 25 mm armoured flight deck. She had four shafts, with turbines of 22,200 shp on the inner pair, and reciprocating engines of 36,200 shp on the outer pair for cruising only. The top speed was 21 knots and she had a range of 7,000 miles at 10 knots. Complement was 875 officers and men.

Though there were three naval air squadrons nominally attached to *Béarn*, they never operated from her. In the opening months of World War 2 the squadrons operated ashore while *Béarn* herself was used as an aircraft transport to bring to France the Douglas A-20 bombers and Curtiss Hawk fighters which had been purchased from U.S.A. for the French Air Force. When France was over-run in June 1940, *Béarn* made for Martinique where she was disarmed and interned. In June 1943, however, Martinique joined the Allied cause and *Béarn* was released. Like the other major French ships she was in urgent need of refitting, and sailed for U.S.A. Here she was completely rearmed with American guns and fire control equipment and then had four single unshielded 5 inch cal. 38 guns, six quad 40 mm AA Bofors guns, and twenty 20 mm Oerlikons. She was also given U.S. Navy boats and radar. Being too slow for use in carrier task forces, *Béarn* was assigned to the more mundane role of aircraft transport and spent the remainder of the war taking new and replacement aircraft across the Atlantic from U.S.A. to Europe – a task shared with several British escort carriers.

The illustration shows *Béarn* in 1944, painted in U.S. Navy style MEASURE 33, a light disruptive camouflage with colours suitable for North Atlantic latitudes.

14. **Le Fantasque:** Destroyer, France

The destroyers of the 'Le Fantasque' class had the distinction of being among the biggest, fastest, and most heavily armed of all vessels in this category. In fact the 'Le Fantasque' class ships were pace-setters in that they started off a new trend towards the 'big' destroyer that was followed by all the other major naval powers by the start of World War 2. By previous standards of size the 'Le Fantasque' class were light cruisers, despite the destroyer classification, or the description *contretorpilleurs* which was the actual French classification of these ships. They were 435 ft long overall, displaced 2,569 tons standard, and up to 3,400 tons full load. Two shaft geared turbines gave 81,400 shp for a designed speed of 37 knots. High speed was a famous feature of these ships. All could steam at 43 knots and one ship of the class, *Le Terrible*, achieved 45¼ knots on trials, exceptionally fast for a ship of this size. Range was 3,000 miles at 14 knots. The armament was five 5·5 inch guns in single mounts, four 37 mm AA guns (two twin mounts), four 13·2 mm AA guns and nine 21·7 inch torpedo tubes in three triple mounts. They were later also fitted for minelaying and could carry fifty mines. The crew numbered 210 officers and men.

The six ships of 'Le Fantasque' class were *Le Fantasque, Le Terrible, Le Triomphant, L'Indomptable, Le Malin,* and *L'Audacieux*. All ordered under the 1930 estimates, *Le Fantasque* was built at at Lorient dockyard, was laid down in November 1931, and launched in March 1934. She was commissioned in March 1936. All the ships had eventful war records. *L'Indomptable, Le Malin,* and *L'Audacieux* took part in the Norwegian campaign in 1940. *Le Fantasque* and *Le Terrible* took part in a number of patrols seeking out the *Graf Spee* in the early months of the war, and sank a German freighter. After the fall of France, *Le*

Fantasque, L'Audacieux, and *Le Malin* sailed for Dakar, and *L'Audacieux* was badly wrecked by gunfire from the cruiser H.M.A.S. *Australia* during the British attack on Dakar in September 1940. Though salved, she never returned to operational service. *Le Malin* was later badly damaged by the Allies at Casablanca, and *L'Indomptable* was interned at Toulon where she was scuttled in November 1942 when the Germans occupied the South of France. *Le Triomphant* was the first of the class to join the Allied cause. She happened to be at the British naval base at Portsmouth in June 1940 when France fell. Her men joined the Free French forces, and *Le Triomphant* subsequently served with British (and later U.S.) naval forces.

Meanwhile *Le Fantasque* and *Le Terrible* were caught up in Dakar, but as soon as Dakar joined the Allies, they were released and sailed to the U.S.A. for a refit at Boston. Later *Le Malin* joined them. Here they were given similar treatment to the other French ships which joined the Allies – American radar and control equipment was fitted, as were extra AA guns, two quad 40 mm Bofors mounts, and ten 20 mm Oerlikons. One

of the torpedo mounts was removed. The three ships then joined the Allied naval forces in the Mediterranean and took part in the landings in the South of France where French ships formed the major part of the naval support. In September 1943 they had similarly assisted at the French liberation of Corsica. Because of the high speed of these ships they were also used for several raids in the Aegean Sea.

The illustration shows *Le Fantasque* as she appeared in 1944, having been painted in the U.S. Navy scheme MEASURE 22, during her American refit.

15. **Aconit**: Corvette, U.K./ France

The British 'Flower' class corvettes became one of the most famous of all warship classes to emerge from World War 2. In the earlier part of the war they bore the brunt of the war against the U-Boat and had the virtue of being relatively cheap and simple so that they could be built quickly. With France and Britain as the two original protagonists against Germany, early plans were made to provide 'Flower' class corvettes for the French Navy. Four ships of the class were earmarked for France, among the earliest of the 'Flowers' laid down in Spring 1940. However, with France falling to Germany in June 1940, these four ships were taken back into British service (though one was mined and lost on sea trials). With the establishment of the Free French (or Fighting French) naval forces, however, eight other 'Flower' class ships building for the Royal Navy were transferred to the Free French on completion in 1941. *Mimosa, Aconit, Roselys, Lobelia, Cdt Dragon, Cdt Detroyat, Alysse,* and *Renoncule* were the French Navy 'Flower' class ships. All served with British escort groups in Atlantic and Russian convoy work. Several of the French corvettes managed to sink U-Boats on their own account. *Aconit* had the most distinguished record of all sinking both U-432 and U-444 in one of the momentous convoy actions of the Battle of the Atlantic. Eastbound convoy HX 228 from Halifax was escorted by the British destroyer *Harvester* and a group of corvettes including *Aconit. Harvester* rammed U-444 on the surface but the submarine got entangled with *Harvester*'s propellers, causing damage to the destroyer. *Aconit* arrived to help and sent U-444 to the bottom by ramming her again. *Aconit* returned to escort the convoy, leaving *Harvester* to limp along behind. *Harvester* was torpedoed and sunk, being almost stationary through the propeller damage, and *Aconit* returned to the scene, obtained a sonar contact on the U-Boat, brought it to the surface with depth charges, and sank this vessel (U-432) by ramming. The captain of *Aconit* at this time was Lieutenant Levasseur.

Like all other 'Flower' class corvettes, *Aconit* displaced 925 tons, was 205 ft in overall length, and her single shaft reciprocating engine gave a top speed of 16 knots. The illustration shows *Aconit* as she appeared at the height of the Battle of the Atlantic. She was painted in the Western Approaches Scheme, basically white and light sea blue, but much affected in this case by the ravages of the heavy seas with which convoy escorts had to contend.

16. **Hova:** Destroyer Escort, U.S.A./France

Once the Lease-Lend scheme came into operation, a number of

U.S. warships were allocated to the Free French forces (as were some British 'River' class frigates). To augment the need for more convoy escort work by the French, six new destroyer escorts of the 'Cannon' class were transferred to the French while still under construction. All commissioned in early 1944, the ships concerned were *Senegalais, Algerien, Somali, Hova, Tunisien,* and *Marocain,* all built by Dravo Shipbuilding Corporation of Wilmington, Delaware. They were known to the French as *torpilleurs d'escortes* and were completely standard DEs of the diesel-electric type, with an electric motor of 6,000 shp giving a top speed of 21 knots on two shafts. They were 1,240 tons standard displacement and 1,650 tons full load. They were 306 ft overall length, $36\frac{1}{2}$ ft beam, and $8\frac{3}{4}$ ft draught. The armament was three 3 inch guns (two forward, one aft), eighteen 20 mm Oerlikons, and one twin 40 mm Bofors. For anti-submarine work the ship was fitted with chutes and throwers aft, and a Hedgehog ahead throwing weapon. Despite coming into service late in the war, all the ships saw action before hostilities ceased. *Senegalais* was damaged while attacking a submarine in the

Mediterranean, but managed to sink the U-Boat which attacked her. All ships were involved in covering the French landings at Provence and *Hova* herself engaged enemy submarines in the Atlantic and was also part of the French Navy Task Force in the Mediterranean in 1944–45. The ships served the French Navy for many years post-war, and further DEs of this type were transferred from U.S.A. to France in 1950.

The illustration shows *Hova*'s 1944 appearance, basically painted in the U.S. Navy's MEASURE 22 camouflage.

17. **Surcouf:** Submarine, France

Of all the submarines involved in operations in World War 2, the French *Surcouf* was the most bizarre and distinctive in appearance. She was an experimental design, rated as a *corsair submarine* (implying that she was a surface raider). In 1939 she was the largest and most heavily armed submarine in the world. She had a surface displacement of 3,304 tons and a submerged displacement of 4,218 tons. She was 360 ft in length and 29 ft in beam. Two diesel motors gave her an 18 knot surface speed, and electric motors gave a submerged speed of $8\frac{1}{2}$ knots. Crew was 118 officers and men. The armament was unique, two 8 inch guns in a barbette forward of the conning tower and a hangar for a light seaplane built into the after end of the structure. A derrick was provided for hoisting the seaplane on and off the water. She had two 37 mm AA guns on the after structure, and had six 21·7 inch torpedo tubes and four 18 inch tubes. She was built to take full advantage of the maximum size and armament for submarines allowed by the Washington Treaty. She was built at Cherbourg and commissioned in May 1934. When France fell in June 1940, *Surcouf* was being refitted at Brest but managed to get to the British naval base at Devonport. Here she was seized – not without casualties – by a British crew, and later handed over to the Free French. She completed her refit in England, then operated in the North Atlantic. She took part briefly in the Free French attack on St. Pierre. In December 1941 the war in the Pacific started, and *Surcouf* was transferred to this area where her long range and big guns could have realised their full potential. How-

ever, she did not reach the Pacific, being sunk in collision with an American freighter as she approached the Panama Canal via the Gulf of Mexico, on 18 February 1942. Thus she had little chance to prove her effectiveness in big ocean warfare.

18.   **Rubis:** Submarine, France

Among all the French ships which managed to escape German clutches and join the Allies in World War 2, the submarine *Rubis* was much the most famous and successful. *Rubis* was one of the 'Saphir' class of six mine-laying submarines built at Toulon dockyard. These ships were of 761 tons displacement (surface) and 925 tons (submerged). The overall length was $214\frac{1}{2}$ ft long and beam $23\frac{1}{4}$ ft. Twin diesel motors of 1,300 shp gave a surface speed of 12 knots and electric motors gave a submerged speed of 9 knots. The armament was one 75 mm gun, one 13·2 mm AA gun, two 21·7 inch torpedo tubes in the bows, and one 21·7 inch and two 15·7 inch tubes in a traversing triple mount aft of the conning tower casing. There was a crew of about forty-two/forty-five men. *Rubis* herself was launched in September 1931 and commissioned in April 1933. The distinctive feature of these boats was their minelaying capability which utilised a new method of submarine minelaying whereby the mines were carried externally in wells, some thirty-two mines making up the full capacity. The depth setting was achieved mechanically. The external carriage of the mines meant that laying was much quicker than the more conventional method of submarine minelaying where the mines are carried internally and launched through a pressure lock. The mines in the 'Saphir' class boats were carried in pairs in eight wells each side which were arranged in fours at each end of the midship ballast tanks.

At the outbreak of war in 1939, *Rubis* was based in the Mediterranean undergoing refit at Bizerta. On completion of this she transferred to Brest with two sister ships for service in northern waters. When Germany moved into Norway in April 1940 the British decided to mine Norwegian territorial waters to disrupt German convoy traffic, and *Rubis* was sent to Dundee to join up with the British 9th Submarine Flotilla. Until June 1940 *Rubis* successfully carried out several minelaying patrols near Bergen, Kristiansund, and

Trondheim. However, the capitulation of France in June 1940 led to the need to decide a future course of events. By the terms of the French Armistice, her warships were to withdraw from operations to designated French ports. The crew of *Rubis* almost unanimously chose to fight on with the Free French forces organised by General de Gaulle, so the ship remained attached to the Royal Navy for operational purposes until the end of the war five years later. She continued patrols in the Norway area, then was refitted early in 1941, mainly to enable her to carry and lay British mines – since French mine stocks were exhausted.

In June 1941 *Rubis* was nearly abandoned when her steering gear jammed and immobilised her, but clever seamanship got her back to port. A further incident only two months later caused her to hit the bottom while avoiding convoy escorts after a successful attack. This caused some damage. For the rest of the war *Rubis* remained extremely active, completing in all some twenty-eight patrols. In October 1943 she laid her 500th mine and by the end of the war had laid 683. Her mines are known to have sunk seven German warships, damaged a U-

Boat, and sunk fifteen cargo ships. She also sunk one cargo ship by torpedo. Her officers and men were awarded numerous British medals and decorations for their skilled and valorous service, and the name of *Rubis* is, indeed, high on the list of submarines which served the Allies well. At various times during the war she sailed from Portsmouth, the Clyde and Dundee, and operated in Norwegian waters, the Bay of Biscay, and along the coast of France. During 1942 a 20 mm Oerlikon gun was fitted in place of the 13·2 mm AA gun aft of the conning tower; she was also given British radar. In peacetime she served with the French Navy until 1956.

Rubis is illustrated as she appeared in the 1940 period. She was later given a pendant number (P.15) in the Royal Navy series, under whose operational control she came, and was then painted in the dark grey scheme of the Royal Navy.

19. **Andrea Doria:** Battleship, Italy

Andrea Doria in 1940 was one of the most modern looking warships in the world, but she was, in fact, already twenty-five years old having been completely transformed in one of the most extensive of reconstructions. She was originally commissioned in 1915 and was a typical battleship of the era – with ram bows, thirteen 12 inch guns (three triple turrets and two twin superfiring turrets), a secondary armament arranged to fire in broadside, and eighteen 3 inch guns. The displacement in 1915 was 22,964 tons standard. By the 1930s, with Mussolini's dreams of an Italian Empire, there was a need to expand the fleet quickly. Some fine new battleships of the 'Roma' class were put in hand, as well as an ambitious scheme to modernise the older battleships to similar modern standards. *Andrea Doria* and her sister ship *Caio Diulio*, together with two near sister vessels, *Conte di Cavour* and *Caio Giulio Cesare*, were subsequently reconstructed to give what amounted to a completely new class of four battleships.

So drastic was the reconstruction that even the engines were changed. In 1915 engines of 32,000 shp gave a top speed of 21½ knots, and the new engines, of 85,000 shp, gave 27 knots. The ram bow was replaced by a clipper bow and an entirely new superstructure with conning tower and control top was installed. The armament was all new, ten 12·6 inch (arranged as two triple and two twin turrets) replaced the original armament, and the new secondary armament was twelve 5·2 in guns (six twin turrets) and ten 3·5 inch guns in single mounts. New funnels and masts completed the transformation. Work on the four ships started in 1935, *Andrea Doria* being taken in hand in April 1937 by Cantieri Riuniti dell' Adriatico at Trieste. She recommissioned again after the reconstruction on 26 October 1940. By this time Italy was already at war with Britain and *Andrea Doria* was blooded in action only days after recommissioning. She had joined the fleet at Taranto and was one of the victims of the famous Taranto raid by Swordfish of the British Fleet Air Arm on the night of 11/12 November 1940. She was slightly damaged by a torpedo, but not sufficiently to interrupt her operations. In December 1941 she was in action as part of the Italian task force which attempted to prevent a convoy to Malta reaching the beleaguered island. This was the convoy escorting the ship *Breconshire* carrying

vital supplies for Malta. The British ships completely outmanoeuvred the Italian attackers, using smoke effectively to conceal their movements and elude the superior Italian force. In February 1941 *Andrea Doria* had been engaged in an Italian force which clashed briefly but indecisively with the famous British Force H, which included *Renown* and *Malaya*, in the bombardment of Genoa.

When the Italian Armistice was signed in September 1943, *Andrea Doria* was at Taranto. With several other ships of the Italian Fleet she sailed for Malta where she remained until June 1944. In the last year of the war she served the Allied cause, though was only involved in minor operations. *Andrea Doria* remained active with the Italian Navy until she was scrapped in 1956. One of her sister ships, *Caio Guilio Cesare*, was handed to the Soviet Navy as a war reparation, becoming the *Novorossisk*. In the rebuilt form, *Andrea Doria* displaced 28,700 tons standard and 29,000 tons full load. She was 612 ft overall and the complement was 1,495 officers and men. The illustration shows *Andrea Doria* in late 1941.

Bartolomeo Colleoni class: Light Cruisers, Italy

Bartolomeo Colleoni was one of a class of four very fast light cruisers which, when first built in the 1931–32 period, set a trend which several other nations later followed. The idea was to produce a ship able to deal with the large 'super destroyers' which France (and soon other nations) were building. So the speed of a light cruiser of this type was a necessity. The four ships of the 'Bartolomeo Colleoni' class had a designed speed of 37 knots, though at least one of them steamed at nearly 40 knots for over eight hours, fully loaded and ready for combat in a pre-war exercise, making these ships probably the fastest cruisers in the world in pre-war years. The four ships in the class were *Bartolomeo Colleoni* herself, *Giovanni Delle Bande Nere*, *Alberico di Barbiano*, and *Alberto di Guissano*. All four ships were sunk by Allied forces in World War 2, the last two together in an enterprising action with one Dutch and three British destroyers early on the morning of 13 December 1941, when the two cruisers were intercepted while escorting a convoy of troopships to North Africa. Despite having superior firepower and speed to the destroyers, the cruisers were swiftly despatched. This action took place off Cape Bon, Tunisia, and the British ships kept close to the shoreline so that their silhouettes were not visible prior to their surprise attack. Significantly this was a night action and Italian ships rarely did well in engagements of this type. The third ship, *Bande Nere*, met her end by torpedo fired from the British submarine *Urge* off Stromboli, on 1 April 1942, and *Bartolomeo Colleoni* became the first major Italian warship to be sunk in a sea battle in World War 2. This happened on 20 July 1940, only a month after Italy had declared war. The Australian cruiser *Sydney* and five destroyers were patrolling the Aegean on the look-out for Italian ships making for the Dodecanese. Four of the destroyers were detached for an anti-submarine patrol off the north of Crete. They spotted two fast cruisers approaching from the west. These were *Bartolomeo Colleoni* and *Bande Nere*. The destroyers withdrew from the superior force and the cruisers gave chase. *Sydney*, over 40 miles away, was radioed by the destroyers and moved to intercept the cruisers. She closed on the two Italian cruisers and in a brisk gun battle set *Bartolomeo Colleoni* on fire and disabled her. *Bande Nere* was damaged but made good her escape, aided by the fact that *Sydney* had nearly exhausted her 6 inch ammunition. The destroyers then went in and sank *Bartolomeo Colleoni*, recovering over 500 survivors as the ship sank. This notable naval victory gave a good boost to British morale when Britain herself was gravely threatened. The drawing shows *G. Delle Bande Nere* as she appeared in March 1942 – after the Italians had started to use camouflage on their warships. The ship was built by Ansaldo Co. at Genoa in 1928–32. She was 555 ft in length, 51 ft beam, and 16½ ft draught. Her turbines gave 95,000 shp, sufficient for over 37 knots. The powerful armament comprised four twin 6 inch turrets, six 3·9 inch AA guns and two 21 inch torpedo tubes.

21.   **Zara:** Heavy Cruiser, Italy

While *Bartolomeo Colleoni* is representative of the Italian light cruisers of World War 2, *Zara* is equally representative of the heavy cruisers. Built exactly to the limits of the Washington Treaty, she displaced the maximum permitted 10,000 tons standard and was constructed by Odero-Terni at Spezia in the 1928–31 period. The four ships of the 'Zara' class were improved 'repeats' of two earlier ships of the 'Trento' class. Much importance was given to the 'Zara' class ships for they would form the backbone of the fleet and supplement the elderly battleships which were otherwise the most powerful units available. While the 'Trento' class had been very lightly armoured, the 'Zara' class had relatively heavy protection at the expense of speed. The side armour belt was 150 mm above the waterline and 100 mm below it. Bulkheads fore and aft were armoured and 120 mm thick, forming an armoured box round the magazines and machinery spaces. Deck armour was up to 70 mm thick with an extra 20 mm layer at some points. Conning tower armour was up to 150 mm. This extensive use of armour plate led the ships initially to be classed as 'armoured cruisers'. The two shaft geared turbines gave 95,000 shp, with a speed of 32 knots. Of all prewar heavy cruisers the 'Zara' class were the most heavily armoured, and were among the most heavily armed, with eight 8 inch guns in four twin turrets. There were sixteen 3·9 inch guns in eight twin turrets, four each side, though the after pair were removed in 1937 and twin 37 mm AA gun mounts replaced them. There were four 40 mm guns and eight 13·2 mm machine guns, by 1940 the 40 mm guns were replaced by a total of eight 37 mm guns. There were no torpedo tubes but an aircraft catapult was mounted on the forecastle, and three aircraft (Ro 43s in 1940) were carried in a hangar below the foredeck. The ships in the class were *Zara, Pola, Fiume,* and *Gorizia.*

In June 1940 *Zara* was the senior ship of the Italian 1st Cruiser Division and she immediately led a sizeable force of cruisers and destroyers in a sweep from Taranto hoping to intercept units of the British Fleet. A British light cruiser and a submarine (which attacked the Italian cruisers) were both sunk in this operation. In July 1940 *Zara* was involved in the famous Battle of Calabria. Ten cruisers and sixteen destroyers made up a screening force for troop transports taking Italian soldiers from Naples to Benghazi. Two cruisers (one of them *Bartolomeo Colleoni*) and many destroyers and torpedo boats comprised the

convoy escort and two battleships, more cruisers, and ten destroyers provided another screening force. All the principal units of the British Mediterranian Fleet were engaged in the bid to stop this heavily escorted convoy. The battle was sharp and fierce and is remarkable for the fact that despite its intensity and the weight of firepower on each side, no ships were lost and there was only minimal damage. A near tragedy occurred, however, when aircraft sent from Italy to support the action bombed Italian ships by mistake, and this led to the adoption of red and white diagonal stripes on the forecastle as a standard air recognition device for all major Italian warships throughout the war. After Calabria *Zara* was involved in several unsuccessful sweeps to seek out British warships. In November 1940 she escaped damage in the Taranto raid.

In March 1941 the Italian Fleet put to sea for a sweep of the Eastern Mediterranean under their commander Vice-Admiral Iachino. The force was split into two, one group led by *Zara* concentrating on the Aegean Sea. On 27 March the force led by *Zara* was ordered to rejoin the main force, led by Admiral

Iachino in the battleship *Vittorio Veneto*. There followed the complex Battle of Matapan which severely mauled the Italian fleet. *Pola*, *Fiume*, and *Zara* were all sunk in this night action. *Pola* had been hit by torpedo in an airstrike during the day. The other ships were caught unexpectedly by H.M.S. *Warspite* as attempts were made to tow *Pola*, and firing at close range, with the targets illuminated by destroyers' searchlights, the British battleship was soon able to destroy and sink all three Italian cruisers, despite a spirited defence by *Zara*. The *Zara*, heavily damaged, was eventually scuttled by her crew to prevent capture of the ship after *Warspite* had reduced the Italian vessel to a burning wreck. Thus ended the career of one of the most famous of all Italian naval vessels. *Zara* is shown as she appeared at the Battle of Matapan.

22. **Vittorio Veneto**: Battleship, Italy

The largest of the Italian Navy's new warship construction in the 1930s was the 'Impero' class, *Impero*, *Roma*, *Littorio*, and *Vittorio Veneto*, which were designed to the maximum limits allowed by the Washington Treaty. They were thus 35,000 tons standard displacement, with nine 15 inch guns in three triple turrets. The secondary armament was twelve 6 inch guns in four triple turrets (disposed one each side, fore and aft), twelve 3·5 inch AA guns in single mounts (six each side), four 4·7 inch (120 mm) guns (to fire star shell), twenty 37 mm AA guns, and sixteen 20 mm AA guns. By 1942 *Vittorio Veneto* had the 20 mm AA armament doubled to thirty-two pieces. *Vittorio Veneto* was laid down in October 1934 (along with *Littorio*) and was launched in July 1937. She was commissioned in April 1940. Four shaft geared turbines gave a speed of 30·5 knots from 130,000 shp. The armour protection included 350 mm in the side belt and turret, 207 mm on the main deck, and 260 mm on the conning tower. The length was 780 ft overall. An aircraft catapult was fitted at the extreme stern with a capacity in a below decks hangar for four Ro 43 aircraft.

These ships were extremely powerful vessels. *Vittorio Veneto* was built at the naval yard at Trieste. She was based at Taranto soon after completion. On the last day of August 1940 *Vittorio Veneto* and *Littorio* led a powerful force of five battleships, thirteen cruisers, and thirty-nine destroyers in a sweep intended to intercept and destroy a British convoy known to be en route from Gibraltar to Alexandria. The force failed to find its quarry however, and was equally unlucky in a similar search a month later. *Vittorio Veneto* escaped serious damage in the great Taranto raid, but was less fortunate on 8 January 1941, when she was damaged in a bombing raid at Naples. At this time *Andrea Doria* was the only Italian battleship fully operational. *Vittorio Veneto* was quickly repaired, however, and in March 1941 she sailed as flagship of Admiral Iachino, the C.-in-C. of the Italian Fleet who was to lead a massive sweep of the Aegean.

There followed the Battle of Gardo Island when the Italian fleet was sought out and engaged by the British fleet. When the battle started *Vittorio Veneto* led the firing on the attacking British cruisers causing them to withdraw, but was soon hit and slowed down by a torpedo dropped by British aircraft. This was a lucky turn of events for the British, for the Italian battle-ship had a great margin of speed and firepower over the cruisers and was fully intent on sinking them. The pursuit of the cruisers by the Italian forces now brought the Italian ships within range of other British ships and this led to the famous Battle of Matapan. There was an air threat from the British aircraft carriers at dusk, and this materialised, resulting in the torpedoing of the accompanying cruiser *Pola*. The Italian fleet was sailing in columns and they put up a great smoke screen as a means of defence. *Vittorio Veneto* was in the middle of the force. Though hit in the afternoon she had by now been well enough repaired to make about 20 knots. By nightfall the British fleet had made contact with part of the Italian force, and the British flagship *Warspite* opened fire at close range on some cruisers (the *Fiume* and *Zara*) which were sunk. The British Commander, Admiral Cunningham, had hoped to engage *Vittorio Veneto* in this action, but the Italian battleship escaped further damage.

The Battle of Cape Matapan was a defeat for the Italian fleet and Italian naval forces did not sweep the sea in such strength again. Subsequently *Vittorio Veneto* saw no more major actions and after the Italian Armistice she was among the ships which operated with Allied forces. She was scrapped in 1948. Of the sister ships, *Roma* was bombed and sunk in September 1943, and *Impero* was never finished, her hull being scrapped in 1947. *Littorio* was renamed *Italia* after the Armistice and was scrapped in 1948. Ironically they were all outlived by the 'Andrea Doria' class ships on which they were intended to be improvements.

23. Kongo: Battleship, Japan

The 'Kongo' class were the oldest of the Japanese battleship force in World War 2, though like some battleships of other nations, they had been considerably rebuilt and modernised in the pre-war period. The original design was British, the nameship *Kongo* being built in a British yard, Vickers-Armstrong, Barrow, though the three subsequent vessels were built in Japanese yards to the same design. Ordered in 1910, when Japan and Britain were allied by treaty, *Kongo* was designed by Sir George Thurston and was based closely on the contemporary Royal Navy *Lion* battle-cruiser,

then under construction. The class was originally rated, in fact, as battle-cruisers, and there was a great similarity in hull form to *Lion*. One major difference, however, was the adoption of 14 inch guns, then the largest calibre in the world, in an attempt to upstage other nations, Britain included. The 14 in guns were designed and built by Vickers. Similarly the secondary armament was made up of 6 inch guns rather than 4 inch guns as in the contemporary British ships.

The four ships of the class, *Kongo, Haruna, Hiei, Kirishima,* were all considerably rebuilt in the inter-war period in the course of successive refits. One ship, *Hiei*, was reduced in armament and power in 1932 to conform to the requirements of the London Naval Treaty, but in 1936 she was refitted and restored to full armament. Among the many alterations incorporated were the change from coal burning to oil, new boilers to give better speed, lengthening of the hull by about 25 ft, anti-torpedo bulges built on to the hull, increased elevation for the guns, and extra deck armour to offer better protection from plunging fire. There was a completely new superstructure which altered the appearance considerably, and the original fore funnel was removed. The bridge was an impressive and prominent 'pagoda'-like structure in characteristic Japanese style and carried a prominent optical fire control system.

By 1940 the ships displaced 31,720 tons standard and nearly 37,000 tons full load. The overall length was 730 ft, the beam 95¼ ft, and draught 32 ft. Four shaft geared turbines of 136,000 shp gave a top speed of 30 knots. The range was 10,000 miles at 18 knots. Armour protection was a belt of 8 inch maximum thickness, plus bulges, 3 inch thickness at bows and stern, 9 inches on the main turrets, 10 inches on the conning tower. The deck armour was 2¾ inches. The armament comprised eight 14 inch guns in four turrets, fourteen 6 inch guns in side casemates, eight 5 inch AA guns, and ten 25 mm AA mounts. The disposition of the main 14 inch turrets was unusual in that the third (super-firing) 14 inch turret was set well forward just aft of the third funnel. This was a novel feature when these ships were first built, since contemporary vessels usually had this turret in a fairly restricted position between the funnels. In the 'Kongo' class all the boiler rooms were grouped together amidships

rather than in two groups fore and aft, and the turret could not therefore be placed between the funnels. It was placed aft of the boiler rooms, giving it a greatly increased arc of fire and giving the ships a good edge in firepower and effectiveness over other ships of the 1910–12 period.

Despite their age, the 'Kongo' class ships were still very efficient and effective fleet units when Japan made her opening move in World War 2. *Kongo* was with her sister ship *Haruna* in the South China Sea in December 1941, forming the main battle squadron. It was to counter-balance the threat of these Japanese battleships that the ill-fated *Repulse* and *Prince of Wales* were sent to strengthen the British fleet at that time, these ships were sunk by Japanese aircraft, however, before any surface action could take place. With the British threat removed, *Kongo* and *Haruna* were then deployed to the Java Sea, joining *Hiei* and *Kirishima*. In March 1942 all four ships joined the carrier task force which engaged the Royal Navy in the Indian Ocean, sinking H.M.S. *Hermes* and other ships.

In June 1942 all four ships were involved in the Battle of

Midway, *Kongo* and *Haruna* covering the invasion fleet. Midway saw the repulse of the Japanese and the islands were not, in fact, invaded. *Kongo* and her sisters were not damaged, however, in the American air attack on the Japanese fleet. When the Americans gained a foothold in Guadalcanal, *Kongo* and *Haruna* took part in a daring close range bombardment of the main American air base at Henderson Field, destroying nearly sixty out of eighty American aircraft and destroying the base facilities. *Kongo* was next involved in the Solomon Islands campaign. In November 1942 both *Hiei* and *Kirishima* were sunk while attempting to repeat *Kongo*'s close-in bombardment of the American base at Henderson, Guadalcanal, for the U.S. Navy had now brought in major surface units to trap any further bombardment attempt.

Guadalcanal was finally abandoned by the Japanese and *Kongo* and *Haruna* returned to Japan for refit. Radar, new triple mount light AA guns, and revised damage control arrangements resulted from this refit, and six of the secondary casemate guns were removed. In June 1944 both ships were at sea for the Battle of the Philippine Sea. Lessons learned here included the need for many more AA guns, and additional twin and single 25 mm mounts were added to bring the total of AA guns to ninety-four. The Battle of Samar in October 1944, saw *Kongo* again in action, and here she and *Haruna* engaged American ships but *Kongo* was herself slightly damaged. In November 1944 with increased Allied air activity, the big ships were recalled to Japan. On 21 November *Kongo* was sunk in the Formosa Straits while heading for Japan, the U.S. submarine *Sealion* carrying out a torpedo raid which caused her to sink very quickly. *Haruna* survived nearly to the war's end but was also sunk, in July 1945, during a carrier-borne air attack near Kure.

The illustration shows the ship as she appeared in 1942. The control top was painted white at this time to render it less conspicuous when the ship was hull down.

24. **Yamato:** Battleship, Japan

Yamato and her equally famous sister ship *Musashi* are well-known as the largest battleships ever built for any navy. They had 18 inch guns as main armament and they were designed and built in blatant disregard of the terms of the Washington and London Naval Treaties. The ships were intended to be superior in firepower and armour to any other battleships in the world. Design work for the ships started as far back as 1934 but much design work was needed before any plans could be finalised. Not the least of the problems was the immense weight of the triple 18 inch turrets, each of which weighed more (2,774 tons) than the average destroyer displacement of the time. The tremendous weight of the main armament, apart from the sheer physical problems of manufacture, meant that the hull had to be built to a greater width and with greater strength than any previous warship.

Five ships were projected of which work on the fifth never started, and work on the fourth was abandoned as an economy measure after the hull had been laid down. *Yamato* and *Musashi* were actually built and commissioned, while the third vessel, *Shinano* was converted while under construction as an aircraft carrier. Many changes were made before *Yamato* herself was laid down in a graving dock at Kure naval yard. One last minute

change was the substitution of the proposed diesel propulsion by steam turbines, since diesels would have posed big maintenance and replacement problems once the armoured decks were in place. The dock had to be deepened, and special new cranes provided before construction could begin. A special dock was built at Yokosuka for the construction of *Shinano*, while *Musashi* was built on a slipway at Nagasaki by the Mitsubishi firm. *Yamato* was started in November 1937. She was launched in August 1940 and commissioned in December 1941. *Musashi* was laid down in March 1937, launched November 1940, and commissioned in August 1942. *Shinano* was altered to a large aircraft carrier during building and was launched in October 1944. On 28 November 1944, she sailed from Yokosuka for Kure to be fitted out, and the next day she was sunk by the U.S. submarine *Archerfish*, so took no part in active operations.

Yamato and *Musashi* were built on a breathtaking scale. They were 863 ft in overall length, 127¾ ft in beam, and had a draught of 35½ ft. The standard displacement was 64,170 tons, or 71,660 tons full load. Four shaft geared turbines gave a top speed of $27\frac{1}{2}$ knots from a power output of 150,000 shp. The armour protection was formidable; 16 inches main side belt, $7\frac{3}{4}$ inches on the main deck, 20/25 inches on the turrets. Torpedo bulges were built in out board of the side armour plate. Because of the vast size a distinctive bulbous bow was featured, this being calculated to reduce hull pressure resistance for a ship of this size. In the years since World War 2, this same type of bulbous bow form has become common in most very large merchant ships, such as super-tankers, whose dimensions in some cases exceed those of *Yamato*. Because of the very large size of the *Yamato* and *Musashi* it was necessary to dredge out some harbours and jetty areas to allow the ships to berth.

When first built the armament was nine 18 inch guns in three triple turrets, twelve 5 inch guns in six twin turrets, twenty-four 25 mm guns in triple mounts, and four 13 mm guns. In succeeding years, however, there were many armament changes. Increased AA protection was a priority requirement and in July 1944 the twenty-five mm guns had been increased to total eighty-seven, while a year later they had further been increased to 146. *Musashi* at the same time had 107 25 mm guns. There was a capacity for four aircraft aft, with two catapults and handling ramps for directing the aircraft on to the catapults. The crew totalled about 2,500 officers and men.

Even by the time they were laid down, the fate of the battleship, as a big gun platform, was sealed, for air power and air attacks showed the vulnerability of a big ship to a determined torpedo assault. Both the *Yamato* and *Musashi* gave good service, however, and survived remarkably well for ships which were sought out as prime targets by the aircraft of the U.S. Navy. *Yamato* became the flagship of Admiral Yamamoto immediately on commissioning. She was soon in action at the Battle of Midway. In August 1942 she was at Truk providing gunfire support for the defence of Guadalcanal. *Musashi* was commissioned at this time and became the fleet flagship, being better fitted out internally for this role. In late 1943 *Yamato* was torpedoed by a submarine and she sustained some flooding. She returned to Kure and at this time the triple 6·1 inch turrets were removed to reduce top weight.

In March 1944 *Musashi* was hit forward by a torpedo from the U.S. submarine *Tunny* and she too returned to Kure for repair. Armament changes – increasing the AA capability – were made at this time. In May 1944 both ships were at Lingga, to the south of Singapore, as part of a large force which was to confront the U.S. Navy in a determined bid to damage the Allied forces. This resulted in the June 1944 Philippine Sea battle which the Japanese lost. In October 1944, when it had been determined to use the firepower of the ships against invasion craft, *Musashi* was sunk in the Sibuyan Sea by massive raids in succession by U.S. Navy aircraft. Some twenty torpedo hits and seventeen bombs were required to finally despatch the great ship, in an action of ferocious intensity. *Yamato* survived this action, but on 25 October, the day after *Musashi*'s sinking, she saw action against a U.S. task force, sinking an escort carrier and a destroyer by gunfire. After this action, the Battle of Samar Gulf, it was decided to withdraw *Yamato* to home waters. In April 1945, with the Allies closing in remorselessly on the Japanese mainland, *Yamato* was sent to lead a 'suicide' fleet against the U.S. forces in Okinawa. On the way, *Yamato* was spotted and then sunk after a tremendous air attack. Seven bombs and eleven torpedoes were needed to finish off this immense ship. The two biggest warships in the world were thus despatched, but not without considerable effort.

25. Akagi: Aircraft Carrier, Japan

As flagship of the Japanese carrier force attacking Pearl Harbor under Admiral Nagumo, *Akagi* was very much involved in the events which brought Japan and the United States to war on 7 December 1941. From her mast was flown the very battle flag which Admiral Tojo had flown at Tsushima in the 1905 battle of the Russo-Japanese war and which was – on 7 December 1941 – flown again as a patriotic symbol of the great operation which the Japanese fleet was now starting. Admiral Nagumo gave the order for take-off from *Akagi*, and from her decks, and five other carriers, came the waves of torpedo bombers, bombers, and fighters which were to deal such a mightly blow to the U.S. fleet anchored unsuspectingly in the safety of Pearl Harbor.

Akagi was a distinctive vessel and the only one of her class, though she had been conceived as one of a class of fast battle-cruisers at the end of World War I, very similar in style, if not appearance, to the British *Hood* of that period. Of the four ships projected, *Amagi, Atago, Takao,* and *Akagi*, only *Akagi* was ever completed. Work on the vessels coincided with the Washington Treaty agreement which limited Japan's capital ship tonnage. *Atago* and *Takao* were immediately abandoned in 1922 and were dismantled while still on the slips. It was decided to convert the more advanced *Amagi* and *Akagi* to aircraft carriers, but part of this plan was frustrated when *Amagi* was very badly damaged in the big Japanese earthquake of September 1923. She was also dismantled incomplete and only *Akagi* was actually launched in April 1925. She was completed in 1927 but was modernised in the 1936–38 period and given a lengthened flight deck which was humped slightly to give aircraft an incline for landing and a slope-away for take-off. The ship betrayed her battle-cruiser ancestry in her handsome, sleek hull lines. In 1941 she displaced 36,500 tons standard, was 855 ft long over-all, 102¾ ft in beam, and 28½ ft in draught. The flight deck was 818 ft long and 100 ft wide. The hull had a belt of 10 inch side armour, and flight deck and hangars were built above the original hull in the form of a superstructure. The four shaft geared turbines gave 133,000 shp, to produce a speed of 31 knots. The armament consisted of six 8 inch guns in casemates aft (relics of the battle-cruiser design), twelve 4·7 inch high angle guns, and twenty-eight 25 mm AA guns. She could carry ninety-one aircraft and had a crew of about 2,000. Four 8 inch guns in the forward casemates were removed in the 1936 refit. *Akagi* had a small navigating and air control bridge to the port side of the flight deck, and a large trunked funnel on the opposite side, canted downwards towards the waterline.

Akagi had only a short period of glory in World War 2, however. After the triumph of the Pearl Harbor raid she was next committed to a major operation in the big force under Admiral Yamamoto which sought to occupy the Midway Islands. *Akagi* was once again the flagship of Admiral Nagumo's carrier task force which also consisted of the carriers *Kaga, Hiryu,* and *Sorya.*

The main U.S. Navy opposition to the Japanese move came from Task Force 16, the carriers *Enterprise* and *Hornet* under the command of Rear Admiral Spruance. The Midway battle was famous for the fact that the opposing ships never came in sight or shot of each other and the entire operation was conducted by means of air strikes between the opposing carrier task forces. On 4 June 1941, the Japanese forces were spotted by a U.S. Navy flying boat from Midway, heading south-east towards the island. Task Force 16 was detailed to intercept and stop the Japanese force, which almost immediately flew off an air strike of 108 aircraft to attack Midway. As this raid was successful, and moreover worthy of a further attack on Midway, Admiral Nagumo made the mistake of flying off his remaining ninety-three aircraft – which had been kept on the carriers for fleet defence – as a second wave strike on Midway. He felt safe in doing so for no enemy naval opposition had been spotted, only American bombers from Midway which were not entirely successful in their mission to attack the Japanese force.

Meanwhile the *Enterprise* and *Hornet* had located and partly estimated the size of the Japanese force and flew off every available aircraft for a major strike. In brilliant weather in the forenoon, the U.S. Navy aircraft found Nagumo's task force defended only by the minimum of air cover from some Zero fighters and some determined AA firepower. The U.S. aircraft pressed home a fierce attack and *Akagi* received a direct hit from a bomb which penetrated the flight deck and exploded in the hangar causing immense ordnance explosions and a fierce fire. *Akagi* had to be abandoned and she was sunk by torpedo from one of her escorting destroyers. In the same raid all of Admiral Nagumo's carriers were sunk, a tremendous victory for the American forces. To some extent it revenged Pearl Harbor, for the best carriers in the Imperial Japanese Navy had been destroyed, a great blow to Japanese pride. It also swung the balance of naval power in the Pacific strongly in favour of the U.S. Navy.

26. **Junyo:** Aircraft Carrier, Japan

Aside from specially built vessels or converted ex-capital ships, the Japanese Navy made provision for taking over other suitable large ships in the event of war for rapid conversion to aircraft carriers. Starting with the *Shoho*, several classes of tanker were developed in which the hull could be rapidly converted to either aircraft carrier, submarine depot ship, or supply ship form. Three liners of the N.Y.K. Line were quickly converted, *Chuyo*, *Taiyo*, and *Unyo*, but these were of very limited value since they lacked such refinements as catapults or arrestor wires. They were brought quickly into service, however, as timely replacements when the best of the Japanese carriers were sunk at Midway. Much the most successful conversions were a further pair, *Hiyo* and *Junyo* which were converted from luxury liners of the N.Y.K. Line. They had been designed in 1939 with provision for aircraft carrier conversion in the basic design. With war seeming very likely, the Japanese naval command purchased the ships late in 1940 while they were still under construction. The liner superstructure, already nearly complete, was dismantled down to deck level and a normal hangar and flight deck built into the hull. The 'liner' outline of the hull was clearly retained. The main deck and hull areas were clad with 25 mm steel to give added protection. The original boilers were replaced, increasing the top speed from 24 to $25\frac{1}{2}$ knots. These ships followed a layout similar to contemporary British and U.S. carriers, featuring an 'island' superstructure to starboard, with a funnel incorporated, in this case canted out to starboard. They were the first Japanese carriers to feature the funnel in this position. Displacement was 24,140 tons, the length $719\frac{1}{2}$ ft, beam $87\frac{3}{4}$ ft, and draught $26\frac{3}{4}$ ft. The flight deck was 690 ft long and $89\frac{1}{2}$ ft wide. Two shaft geared turbines gave 56,250 shp at the top speed of $25\frac{1}{2}$ knots. The armament included twelve 5 inch AA guns in six twin mounts and twenty-four 25 mm AA guns. There were fifty-three aircraft and the crew was about 1,200 men.

Junyo commissioned in May 1942 and took part in the Battle of Santa Cruz in October 1942 as one of four carriers in Admiral Yamamoto's Combined Fleet which was supporting Japanese forces on Guadalcanal. In the air strikes which followed two of the Japanese carriers were badly damaged, leaving *Junyo* and *Zuikaku* to launch a counter strike against the U.S. fleet. Aircraft from *Junyo* damaged the battleship *South Dakota* and the cruiser *San Juan*. In the summer of 1943, *Junyo* was torpedoed in the stern while proceeding through the Bungo Strait. Repaired at Kure, she then took part in the Marianas (Philippine Sea) battle where her aircraft had little success and were lost in large numbers during the famous 'Turkey Shoot'. Her sister *Hiyo* was sunk in this battle and *Junyo* herself was slightly damaged. Returning to Kure she was refitted to give added protection. Additional 25 mm AA guns were added (bringing the total to forty), and concrete protection was added round the aviation fuel tanks. Six 12 cm rocket projectors were fitted on the port and starboard bows. In December 1944 she was torpedoed in the stern by the U.S. submarine *Redfish* and so badly damaged as to be laid up for the rest of the war. She was finally broken up in 1947.

The illustration shows her in 1942 in the overall dark grey colour applied to several Japanese carriers at the time.

27. **Myoko:** Heavy Cruiser, Japan

The 'Myoko' class were all built as heavy cruisers under the terms of the Washington Treaty limitations which imposed an upper limit of 10,000 tons displacement and 8 inch guns as main armament. The 'Myoko' class ships were cleverly designed (by Admiral Hiraga, a prominent Japanese naval architect) to take full advantage of space and power to make them among the most powerful and fastest heavy cruisers afloat. The four ships in the class were *Myoko, Nachi, Ashigara*, and *Haguro*, all except *Myoko* being sunk during the war years. *Myoko* was built at Yokosuka yard and completed in 1929. Some modifications to all ships took place in 1936, involving armament and structural changes. By 1941 the displacement had been increased to 13,380 tons. The length was $661\frac{1}{4}$ ft, the beam 68 ft, and the draught $20\frac{3}{4}$ ft. Four shaft geared turbines gave 130,250 shp, top speed being $33\frac{3}{4}$ knots. There was an inclined armour belt of 3/4 inches and a further torpedo bulkhead inboard. The armament was ten 8 inch guns, five twin turrets, eight 5 inch, eight 25 mm AA, four 13 mm AA, and eight torpedo tubes in two quadruple mounts. Catapults were fitted for two aircraft. During the course of the war the AA armament was greatly augmented, up to fifty-two 25 mm guns in twin, triple, and single mounts.

Myoko was Admiral Takagi's flagship at the Battle of the Coral Sea, in May 1942, Takagi being the carrier task group commander. At Guadalcanal in October 1942, *Myoko* was one of the cruisers shelling American positions ashore. In one night shoot she and another cruiser fired over 800 8 inch rounds. At Bougainville in October and November 1943, *Myoko* was again a flagship and in a bitterly fought night action at Empress Augusta Bay she fatally damaged one of her own destroyer screen in a collision. At Leyte Gulf in October 1944 she was badly damaged in the Sibuyan Sea and in December was torpedoed off Jacques Point. Her stern was damaged and she was immobilised. She remained at Singapore for repairs but was still there inactive when the war ended. The illustration shows the ship as she was at Leyte Gulf in 1944.

28. **Fubuki**: Destroyer, Japan

Japanese destroyers fought hard and well against great odds in World War 2 and losses were very high. It is almost invidious to pick out individual ships for there were many notable actions. However, *Fubuki* stands out as name ship of a class which set the pace in all destroyer development in the inter-war period, and *Fubuki*'s design influenced the design of many other destroyers. The 1922 Washington Naval Treaty limitations caused the Japanese Navy to think hard about maximising the permitted characteristics and tonnage, and destroyers superior to those of all rival powers became a major part of the policy. Until this time destroyers generally displaced between 1,000 and 1,400 tons, but by 1925 the Japanese Navy had designed something much bigger, displacing 1,680 tons, 388 ft long overall, 34 ft in beam, and $10\frac{1}{2}$ ft draught. Twin shaft geared turbines of 50,000 shp gave a top speed of 38 knots. The armament was considerably in excess of that then carried in other destroyers. There were three twin 5 inch mounts, one forward and two aft (with one superimposed). The mounts were fully enclosed turrets, all gas-tight. The hull was structurally light, but very well shaped with high forward freeboard and flare to give good sea-keeping qualities. Much thought went into this aspect, so that, for instance, the engine room air intakes were set high to keep them clear of seas breaking over the deck. Nine 24 inch (61 cm) torpedo tubes in three triple mounts were provided, with reload stowage lockers each side of the aft funnel and to port of No. 2 mount. The combination of size, speed, range (5,000 miles), and armament was so far in advance of any previous Japanese destroyer that the class was known as the 'Special Type Destroyer' or 'Fubuki Specials' after the name of the first ship, *Fubuki*. The *Fubuki* was built at Kosakubu yard, launched in November 1927 and completed in August 1928. She was the first of nine ships, all commissioned in the 1928–29 period.

The appearance of this radical new and powerful design had a profound effect on all the other major powers. U.S.A., France, Russia, and Italy all built ships of comparable size and type in the years that followed, with Britain following a similar trend in the late 1930s with the 'Tribal' class destroyers.

Aside from the powerful gun arrangement, the torpedo equipment was superior to any other nations, particularly after 1933 when the famous oxygen-driven 'Long Lance' type 93 torpedo came into use. This had a range of over 43,000 yards and a warhead of 1,100 lb. All the torpedo tubes could be reloaded for firing in only 15 minutes.

The 'Fubuki' class ships were not without faults. The vast number of heavy weapons carried made them top heavy and two ships lost their bows while one ship was nearly rolled over in a big storm in 1935. This led to immediate modifications with the addition of hull reinforcing plates and ballast low down in the hull which increased the displacement to 2,090 tons and reduced the top speed to 34 knots. There were other changes to the first group of 'Fubuki' class. When first built all the gun and torpedo stations were linked to the bridge by distinctive voice pipes but from 1935 these were removed and replaced by a telephone system. With the coming of World War 2 there were armament changes, mainly to improve the anti-aircraft capability. The No. 2 turret was removed and six 25 mm guns took its place, while up to eight more 25 mm guns were also fitted. The first group of 'Fubuki' ships also had their two remaining twin 5 inch turrets (elevation 40 deg.) replaced by later pattern turrets with high elevation (75 deg.) 5 inch guns which could be used against aircraft. These later type guns and turrets were fitted as built into the repeat classes of 'Fubuki' ships. For in addition to the first ten ships there was a second group of ten ships built in the 1929–32 period, and a third group of four ships completed in 1932–33. These latter ships had a narrow fore funnel since they had one boiler room fewer than the earlier ships.

One destroyer of the first group was sunk in a collision in 1934, but all the others formed the backbone of the Japanese destroyer fleet when Japan declared war on America. Only two ships of the entire group survived the war in 1945. The others fell victim to American guns, bombs, and torpedoes as they were involved in virtually every major naval action of the Pacific war. *Fubuki* herself was sunk in a typical engagement, the Battle of Cape Esperance, on the night of 11/12 October 1942. *Fubuki* and a sister ship *Hatsuyuki* were escorting three cruisers in a bombardment group which were covering another force attempting to land men and supplies at Guadalcanal. The approach of these ships was seen in daylight by an American reconnaissance

plane and a U.S. task force of five destroyers and four cruisers awaited the oncoming Japanese force off Cape Esperance as they approached near midnight. In the ensuing running battle *Fubuki* was wrecked by gunfire and torpedoed. One of the cruisers was also sunk and the others damaged before they withdrew.

29. **Yukikaze**: Destroyer, Japan

The three groups of 'Fubuki Specials' were followed by the 'Hatsuharu' class which were similar in appearance but reduced in length to keep them to new limitations of displacement imposed by the London Naval Treaty of 1931, 1,400 tons. The length was $359\frac{1}{2}$ ft overall. The armament and its disposition (five 5 inch guns – two twin mounts and a single) – almost matched that of the 'Fubuki' class. The ships were top heavy and most unstable, however, and an instant programme of modification was needed, reducing both the armament and the superstructure. Two further types followed, the 'Shiratsuyu' and 'Asashio' classes, which were of the 'compact' type like the 'Hatsuharu' class but modified to help overcome the stability problems previously encountered. In 1937, however, Japan opted out of the London Naval Treaty agreement and was thus free to revert to the larger type of destroyer like the 'Fubuki' class.

This led to the 'Kagero' class of eighteen ships which were built in the 1938–40 period, having been authorised under the 1937 naval estimates. The 'Kagero' class represented the high point of Japanese destroyer design, and they were the most formidable in the world at the time of their introduction. Essentially the 'Kagero' class were derived directly from the 'Fubuki' design with some features from the 'Asashio' class. As designed the 'Kagero' class displaced 2,033 tons, were 388¾ ft long overall, 35½ ft in beam, and drew 12½ ft. In order to meet naval staff requirements a range of 5,000 miles at 18 knots was needed and this was comfortably achieved by the 'Kageros', giving them excellent 'long legs' for Pacific operations. Twin-shaft geared turbines of 52,000 shp gave a top speed of 35 knots. There were six 5 inch guns in three twin turrets, four 25 mm AA guns, two 13 mm guns, and eight 24 inch torpedoes in two quadruple mounts.

Modifications to the original 'Fubuki' design included a less rounded stern and 'cleaner' hull, more streamlined bridge and funnels, and lower set torpedo tubes. Extensive welding was used to save weight, and the fuel consumption was reduced compared to the 'Fubuki' class. As originally produced the 'Kagero' class had two 5 inch turrets, two aft, one forward, but the anti-aircraft armament was poor and once the war started there were some extensive changes. The No. 2 (superimposed) turret was removed, and replaced by 25 mm AA guns, while further AA guns were added forward of the bridge. The 'Kagero' class proved a sensation when first commissioned, and one direct result was that the U.S. Navy designed the 'Fletcher' class destroyers (see *Nicholas*) to produce a ship of comparable range and firepower. One area in which the Japanese destroyers were inferior was in the provision of radar and sonar, which was of limited performance. Indeed radar was not fitted when the ships were new in 1940–41.

With the exception of *Yukikaze*, all ships of the 'Kagero' class were sunk during the war years, an indication of the extremely harsh nature of the

Japanese–American naval war in the Pacific. *Yukikaze* survived the war with one of the most distinguished records of all Japanese ships. *Yukikaze* was built at Sasebo and on commissioning in January 1940 she joined the crack 2nd Destroyer Squadron. In the early part of the war she supported landings in the Philippines and Celebes and was not involved in any hostile actions. In February 1942, however, she took part in the victorious Battle of the Java Sea in which a strong Allied force was decisively vanquished. A few days after this *Yukikaze* shelled and sank a cruising U.S. submarine, U.S.S. *Perch*. For the Battle of Midway *Yukikaze* transferred to the 10th Destroyer Squadron, part of the screening force for the Combined Fleet. In the Battle of the Solomon Islands, *Yukikaze* was present at the sinking of the U.S. carrier *Hornet*, and she was part of the bombarding force at Guadalcanal. Here she fired over 370 rounds of 5 inch ammunition and is believed to have sunk two U.S.N. destroyers. After this action *Yukikaze* rescued survivors from the damaged battleship *Hiei* and then torpedoed the stricken ship.

In January 1943 she was involved in the Japanese withdrawal from Guadalcanal, in a series of small actions. A refit in May 1943 resulted in *Yukikaze* receiving radar and having the AA armament augmented. In July 1943 she was involved in the Battle of Kula Gulf where ten Japanese destroyers and three light cruisers inflicted great damage on a U.S. Navy cruiser and destroyer task force. Three U.S. cruisers were badly damaged and a destroyer was sunk. A further refit in August 1943 resulted in the No. 2 turret being removed in favour of light AA guns. Radar was augmented and improved at the same time. Most of the next year was spent in escorting naval supply ships until October 1944 when *Yukikaze* joined a task force attempting to attack U.S. carriers in the Philippines. An American escort carrier and a destroyer were sunk by gunfire in this action, but the Japanese ships did not achieve their object of sinking attack cruisers. The Japanese ships withdrew to Brunei, Borneo, then later sailed to Japan. *Yukikaze* escorted the battleship *Kongo* on this journey, but *Kongo* was torpedoed by a U.S. submarine en route.

In November 1944 *Yukikaze* was escorting the giant new carrier *Shinano* on her maiden voyage when the carrier was sunk spectacularly by the U.S. submarine *Archerfish*. In April 1945, another naval defeat was inflicted when the big battleship *Yamato* was sunk near Okinawa by U.S. bombers. *Yukikaze*, one of the escorts, survived this attack. When Japan surrendered in August 1945, *Yukikaze* remained in full fighting trim anchored at the port of Maizuru. She was at once pressed into service as a repatriation ship taking Japanese ex-prisoners of war back to Japan, and for this role her armament was unshipped. In July 1947 she was handed over to the Chinese Navy as a war reparation where she was renamed *Tang Yan*. She was wrecked in May 1970 during a typhoon.

30. **I-168**: Submarine, Japan

The Japanese developed a wide range of submarines in the inter-war period, some of their designs being based closely on the contemporary British 'L' class, and others on the later large U-Boats of the German Navy in 1918. Japanese policy for submarine deployment was to use them as part of the strength of fleet task forces with the result that only quite rarely did they achieve success, at least in terms of the relatively large numbers of submarines available. It was infrequent for submarines to operate, either singly or in groups, away from fleet command, but on those occasions when they did they invariably proved quite successful. The most widely used type of Japanese submarine was the 'Kaidai' or 'cruiser' type. The first of these was *I-52* designed and built in the 1920–22 period, copied from a German design of 1918, and *I-51* based on a British design. By the later 1920s there had appeared the 'I-53' class, a definitive production 'Kaidai' type. The 'I-64' and 'I-65' classes were repeat boats with only minor changes. In the 1932–35 period a further class of 'Kaidai' boats appeared, the 'I-68' class, which was a further repeat of the same basic design but with detail improvements and slight enlargement.

The surface displacement was 1,400 tons, and the underwater displacement was about 2,000 tons. The overall length was $343\frac{1}{2}$ ft, the beam 27 ft, and draught 15 ft. Two-shaft diesel motors of 9,000 shp gave a good surface speed of 23 knots while electric batteries gave an underwater speed of 8 knots. On the surface these boats could move at 10 knots for over 14,000 miles. The diving depth was up to 250 ft. The armament was a 3·9 inch AA gun on the forward casing, though the last three boats in the class had a 4·7 inch gun instead. There was a roomy enclosed conning tower. The crew numbered seventy. The five ships of the class were numbers *I-68* to *I-73* originally, but from May 1942 '100' was added to the numbers – thus *I-68* became *I-168*.

The class 'I-168' was the most successful and her great moment came on 6 June 1942, at the Battle of Midway. The combined fleet under Admiral Yamamoto had a submarine screen of no less than sixteen boats moving ahead of it. When the U.S. fleet was engaged by Japanese carrier aircraft, however, the Japanese submarines were not heading in the right direction and contact was not made. However, a successful raid by Japanese carrier bombers crippled the carrier *Hornet* and she was abandoned, believed to be sinking. *Hornet* stayed afloat for more than a day, however, and a belated attempt was made to take her in tow. While this was happening the Japanese submarines had made contact once more with the

U.S. Task Force; *I-68* successfully stalked *Hornet*, and sank her with two torpedoes, then torpedoed the destroyer *Hammann* which was standing by *Hornet*. *I-168*, as she then was, was unlucky herself, however, and in July 1943 she was sunk by the U.S. submarine *Scamp*. A sister ship of *I-168*, *I-70* was sunk by aircraft from U.S.S. *Enterprise* while en route to Pearl Harbor on the evening of 7 December 1941, having been instructed to reconnoitre the area.

31. **San Demetrio:** Tanker, U.K.

San Demetrio was one of the first merchant ships in World War 2 to become very widely known by name, the adventures of this tanker coming very early on in the war to symbolise the courage of the merchant seamen who were bringing food and materials to beleaguered Britain. A motor driven tanker of 8,073 tons gross, 4,815 tons net, she was 463 ft long, and was powered by a 502 hp Kincaid oil engine which drove a single shaft and gave a top speed of 12 knots, fully laden in smooth weather. Cargo capacity was about 12,000 tons of gasoline. The owners were Eagle Oil and Shipping Co., and in 1940 *San Demetrio* was a fairly new and modern ship. She was engaged in shipping gasoline from the Dutch West Indies to Britain. After a refit in Tilbury Docks, London, where among other things, degaussing gear was added, on 1 October 1940, she arrived at Aruba in the Dutch West Indies to take on cargo, having been convoyed uneventfully across the Atlantic. From Aruba the loaded tanker sailed north to Halifax, Canada, arriving on 20 October 1940, and sailed in a convoy bound for the River Clyde which departed Halifax on 28 October.

This convoy, of some thirty-seven ships, six of them tankers, sailed at a time when Britain's warships were fully stretched and in short supply. Because of this shortage there was only one escort vessel available, the armed merchant cruiser H.M.S. *Jervis Bay*. This ship had virtually no anti-submarine capability, but there was also a threat at the time on the American side of the Atlantic of surface raiders, for which *Jervis Bay* was, theoretically at least, better armed. A passing convoy heading for Halifax reported submarine activity and had lost four ships. *San Demetrio* was forced to stop to effect engine repairs and rejoined the convoy after steaming at top speed on 5 November 1940. Later that day the German pocket battleship *Scheer* came upon the convoy and opened fire, being gallantly challenged by *Jervis Bay* which was quickly sunk by gunfire. *Scheer* could then pick off the remaining ships at will. In the confusion which followed several ships escaped from the convoy. *San Demetrio* was hit early on, however, and caught fire. Since the cargo had a low flash point, the captain ordered the burning vessel to be abandoned, and the crew took to the boats. By now all the midship superstructure was ablaze. Through the night the lifeboats rode out a gale and were soon parted from the scene of action. A passing ship was sighted by one of the lifeboats but failed to see the occupants.

The next afternoon the men in the same lifeboat spotted another ship, which as they approached was recognised as the *San Demetrio* which they had left the previous day. She was now drifting and still burning, but the sea was still too rough for any attempt at reboarding. For the next night the lifeboat managed to keep close to *San Demetrio* and the next forenoon the lifeboat was sailed up to leeward and the crewmen managed to reboard – by now suffering from the effects of two days in a lifeboat in cold weather. Attempts to secure the lifeboat ended in the boat being swept away, so now the men were forced to stay aboard *San Demetrio* with only a small wooden dinghy left on the ship.

The ship was in a severely damaged condition with most of the upperworks gutted by fire and one fuel tank burning. The crewmen did their best to rehabilitate the vessel. The engine room was bailed out, and the degaussing generator was started up to provide electric power for the services. One of the auxiliary boilers was also started, providing power for the pumps and the firemain. By 8 November the fires were out and the engine started up. Steering had to be done from the remaining hub of the emergency steering wheel aft (since the bridge was wrecked) and a system of lights was rigged up to convey engine room telegraph orders. White paint was used to mark 'S.O.S.' and 'HELP' on the remains of the superstructure, and the ship herself was headed slowly and alone for England. There was no navigation equipment left and the

second officer, the senior of the men on board, had to navigate entirely by guesswork. One man died as a result of injuries and exposure, and the going was tough for there was little edible food remaining on the ship.

On 12 November, however, just a week after the *Scheer* action *San Demetrio* made a landfall off Blacksod Bay, Co. Mayo, Ireland. Once spotted, she was joined by a tug, a destroyer, and air cover. With food put aboard she sailed under her own steam for the Clyde, arriving at Rothesay on 16 November. The crewmen who brought her in received salvage money, and the ship was repaired and put back into service, though she was sunk in another convoy just two years later.

32. **Jervis Bay:** Armed Merchant Cruiser, U.K.

In the early part of World War 2, the British Navy augmented their shortage of surface ships by commissioning a number of requisitioned passenger liners as armed merchant cruisers, repeating an expedient of World War 1. These ships were much used as convoy escorts, and were expected to be useful as a deterrent to surface raiders. Most famous of the British armed merchant cruisers was H.M.S. *Jervis Bay*, a twin-screw vessel of 14,164 tons gross which had been built in 1922 as an emigrant ship plying between Australia and England. The top speed was 15 knots. When war was declared in 1939 she was under the flag of the Aberdeen and Commonwealth Line and was taken over immediately by the Royal Navy. She was fitted with eight 6 inch guns and two 3 inch guns. She was 548½ ft long, 68¼ ft in beam, and drew 33¼ ft. Like all the ex-liners used as armed merchant cruisers, *Jervis Bay* was roomy and had a long range. She was one of fifty-six vessels originally requisitioned, though the idea of using armed merchant cruisers was abandoned when their extreme vulnerability was demonstrated. By late 1941, fifteen had been sunk for they were no real match for either submarine or surface raiders.

The action in which *Jervis Bay* was involved came about on 4 November 1940, when she was the sole escort of a Halifax–Clyde convoy which had left Halifax on 28 October 1940. This was the convoy in which *San Demetrio* was one of the thirty-seven ships. *Jervis Bay* was commanded by Captain Fogarty Fegen, R.N., an officer with distinguished service in World War 1. The convoy commodore was embarked in S.S. *Cornish City*, and the largest ship in convoy was the New Zealand Shipping Co.'s M.V. *Rangitiki*. At 1800 hours on 5 November, the German pocket battleship *Scheer* caught the convoy and opened fire at about ten miles range with her 11 inch guns, picking out *Rangitiki*, the biggest target. The convoy was ordered to scatter by the commodore, making smoke.

Jervis Bay then turned to steam straight at *Scheer*, though *Scheer* still had time to hit and set afire *San Demetrio*. *Jervis Bay* meanwhile closed with *Scheer*, though greatly outranged and outmatched in armament. The merchant cruiser was soon hit on the bridge, her main steering gear was destroyed, and the forward 6 inch guns put out of action. With only limited steering ability it then became difficult to bring the remaining 6 inch guns to bear. After continual hits the bridge area was set on fire, and all but one lifeboat were shot to pieces. The *Jervis Bay* quickly settled in the water and then sank stern first, taking Captain Fegen with her. Survivors were picked up after dark by a Swedish ship *Stureholm* which had scattered with the rest but stayed in the vicinity. Fegen's act in engaging *Scheer* had diverted the German ship's attention from the convoy and no less than thirty-three of the thirty-seven ships reached Britain safely, among them *San Demetrio* whose story is told above.

Captain Fogarty Fegen was subsequently awarded a posthumous Victoria Cross for his action. Only sixty-five members of the crew survived, some 190 dying in the action or from exposure after abandoning ship.

Jervis Bay is illustrated and described in her pre-war role in *Merchant Ships of the World in Colour, 1910–1929.*

33. **Sydney:** Light Cruiser, Australia

The most modern of the Royal Australian Navy's major warships at the start of World War 2 were the cruisers *Sydney*, *Perth*, and *Hobart*; originally built for the Royal Navy as *Phaeton*, *Amphion*, and *Apollo* but transferred to Australia. The class as a whole was known as the 'Modified Leander' class, for the design was based on the Royal Navy's 'Leander' class ship (which in-cluded the famous *Ajax* and *Achilles*) and the ships were built as 'repeats' of the original class.

A very distinctive difference existed, however, in that while the 'Leander' class had a very prominent single trunked funnel, the 'Modified Leander' class had two widely spaced funnels. This was caused by a rearrangement of the machinery spaces. In the 'Leander' class the boiler rooms were adjacent but in the 'Modified Leander' class the boiler and engine rooms were spaced alternately to obviate the risk of immobilising the ship with one hit affecting both boiler rooms as was possible with the original 'Leander' ships. The 'Modified Leander' ships were 555 ft long overall, $56\frac{3}{4}$ ft in beam and drew $15\frac{3}{4}$ ft. The displacement was 6,830 tons and the four shaft geared turbines of 72,000 shp gave a top speed of $32\frac{1}{2}$ knots. The main armament was eight 6 inch guns in four turrets, disposed conventionally, two turrets forward, two aft. The secondary armament was eight 4 inch guns in four twin shielded mounts, arranged two turrets each side amidships. One Walrus amphibian aircraft was carried, with a catapult and crane between the two funnels. The crew totalled

550 officers and men. There were eight 21 inch torpedo tubes in two quadruple mounts, and the light AA armament consisted of twelve 0·5 inch machine guns, on three quadruple mounts. The armour protection was a side belt of 2/4 inches, a deck armour of 2 inches, and main turret armour of 1 inch.

Sydney was built by Swan Hunter of Wallsend in 1933–35. She was with the British Mediterranean Fleet when Italy declared war on Britain in June 1940, and she won early fame when she helped sink the Italian cruiser *Bartolomeo Colleoni* on 19 July 1940. This was the action in which the Italian cruiser gave chase to four British destroyers which led her within range of *Sydney*, patrolling unknown to the Italians just a short way off. Very quick and accurate shooting by *Sydney* hit *Bartolomeo Colleoni* in the engine room, slowing her up sufficiently for the destroyers to make a torpedo attack. Other actions in the Mediterranean in which *Sydney* was involved included the sinking of the Italian destroyer *Espero* in June 1940, the Battle of Calabria in July 1940, and a bombardment of enemy torpedo boat bases in the Dodecanese Islands in September 1940.

In early 1941 she left the Mediterranean Fleet and returned to Australian waters. On 19 November 1941, she met her end in action with the German surface raider *Kormoran*. This was one of the German 'special service' ships, which were disguised as merchantmen and had a powerful concealed armament. *Sydney* spotted *Kormoran* and sailed close to examine what appeared to be an unidentified merchant vessel off the coast of Australia. As *Sydney* closed up on *Kormoran*, the German ship dropped her disguise and opened fire with her five concealed 9 inch guns. This salvo immediately wrecked *Sydney*'s bridge. *Sydney*'s guns replied and destroyed *Kormoran*'s engine room and set her on fire. *Kormoran* was able to get in one more salvo and a torpedo hit before both ships, now each immobilised, drifted apart. *Kormoran*'s ship's company abandoned ship just before it blew up, and the lifeboats took them into captivity in Australia. *Sydney* was never seen again and is believed to have blown up when the fires spread to the magazines. There were no survivors.

An equally brave record was held by *Sydney*'s sister ship *Perth*. She also served in the

Mediterranean, taking part in the Cape Matapan action and the evacuation of Crete in May 1941. She was involved in the famous Battle of the Java Sea, Dutch East Indies, on 28 February 1942, when she was sunk by Japanese ships. *Perth* was one of five cruisers in the A.B.D.A. (American-British-Dutch-Australian) Force under the Dutch Admiral Karel Dorrman. The squadron, with destroyer escort, steamed to cut off a force of Japanese naval ships and troop transports approaching Java. This force proved to be greatly superior to the A.B.D.A. force, and the action which followed resulted in sinkings and damage to the A.B.D.A. ships. During the night which followed, *Perth* received some damage and pulled into the port of Tanjong Priok, Batavia, to attempt essential repairs. She left on the night of 28 February, and sailed for the Sunda Strait, with U.S.S. *Houston*, where a Japanese amphibious force was spotted in Banten Bay. One of the Japanese escorting destroyers, *Fubuki*, attempted to torpedo the two Allied cruisers but missed and her torpedoes sank two of the Japanese troop transports. Passing through the strait, *Perth* and *Houston* then encountered

the heavy cruisers *Mogami* and *Mikuma*, which engaged them at very close range with their 8 inch guns. Just after midnight *Perth* sank from the effects of gunfire and a torpedo hit. *Houston* sank half an hour later.

The third ship of the class, *Hobart*, had a less eventful war, and became a training ship after 1945, eventually being scrapped in 1962.

34. S-10: Motor Torpedo Boat, Germany

The stern limitations of the Versailles Treaty had reduced Germany's navy to a modest size, and certain types were completely prohibited. The first vessel of the motor torpedo boat type was initially designated a 'Wachboot' ('guard boat') to disguise its function, since coastal craft were allowed for patrol work but not for offensive purposes. This first boat, W1, was built by the firm of Lürssen of Bremen who had good experience of building civilian motor boats and offshore cruisers. This vessel was completed in August 1930 and became the prototype for all subsequent S-Boat classes, establishing the classic layout of this type of craft with its torpedo tubes mounted high on the bow.

In 1932 W1 was re-designated S I (Schnell Boot), and the experience gained with the vessel led to refinements of design which were incorporated in the first full production class. S I had an open bridge/steering position which was subsequently enlarged and enclosed on later craft. Three Daimler-Benz gasoline engines of 900 hp drove S I at a top speed of 32 knots. It was soon realised that these boats constituted a fire risk, and the firms of MAN and Daimler were asked to develop large diesel motors suitable for S-Boat use.

The first four production boats, however, S-2 to S-5 still had gasoline engines, though an innovation was a Maybach 100 hp engine which could be clutched into the centre of the three propeller shafts to give 'silent' running facility for cruising at 6 knots. Other new features were an enclosed bridge and heating. S-6, S-7, and S-9 followed in 1934, these having the new Maybach L-7 diesel engines. Though these boats were slightly heavier than the earlier boats, displacing 80 tons, there was no improvement in speed even though this was anticipated, as the new engines were themselves much heavier than the old gasoline motors. In the next batch built, S-10 to S-13, a further improvement was the incorporation of a knuckle in the bow to keep the forecastle rather drier than on the earlier boats. The Daimler-Benz MB 502 16 cylinder diesel motor was fitted in this group, each of the three motors delivering 1,320 hp. This motor proved very reliable and successful and no more MAN engines were ordered. In the S-10 type S-Boats the displacement was 78 tons, the hull length 106 ft 4 inches, beam 16 ft, and draught $5\frac{1}{2}$ ft. There were two torpedo tubes mounted on the forecastle with one reload for each tube carried on deck behind each tube. On the after deck was a single 20 mm AA gun. The complement was sixteen/ twenty men. The S-10 type boats were completed in 1935–36, all built by Lürssen. Composite construction was used throughout, the hull being mahogany over metal framing, with an inner skin of cedar.

After war was declared in September 1939, S-10 was part of the 2nd S-Boat Flotilla based at Heligoland, though in 1940 when a flow of new construction S-Boats began to appear, S-10 and her other early sister ships were withdrawn for use as training vessels. S-10 is representative of the early S-Boat design and the drawing shows her appearance in the closing months of 1939, painted in the very pale grey adopted for S-Boats as a standard colour. Pre-war exercises showed that this colour gave them the best concealment under both day and night conditions.

35. **S-195:** Motor Torpedo Boat, Germany

There were still only eighteen S-Boats in the Kriegsmarine when World War 2 started, but a steady programme of new construction led to a continuing increase in S-Boat strength. A major area of S-Boat activity, particularly in the 1940–41 period, was a series of attacks on British coastal convoys off the east and south coasts of England. There were numerous sinkings of small British freighters in a series of fast 'hit-and-run' raids. To the British the area became popularly known as 'E-Boat Alley'. Some twenty-five British merchantmen, plus some warships, were sunk by S-Boats in 1940. In the latter half of 1941 there were at first several suc-

cessful operations in the Baltic following the German invasion of Russia. S-Boats were also used quite extensively for mine-laying here. Emphasis on this area of operations left fewer S-Boats to harass British shipping, but even so about thirty British coastal ships were sunk during 1941 by S-Boat action alone. Two flotillas of S-Boats moved to the Mediterranean in late 1941, one early task being to mine the approaches to Grand Harbour, Malta. Further operations were based on the North African coast in support of the Afrika Korps until North Africa fell when the surviving boats moved to Italy. A few of the older S-Boats were transported overland to provide a flotilla for the Black Sea and they operated in that theatre with some success until August 1944 when the area was entirely over-run by the Soviets and the surviving boats were scuttled.

The best operating area for S-Boats remained the English Channel and North Sea, however, where significant numbers of British merchantmen and small warships were sunk and much minelaying work was carried out. The first big set-back to S-Boat operations came in 1944 when there was greatly increased

Allied air and naval activity in connection with the Normandy invasion. Some fifteen S-Boats were sunk in a single night during an air-raid on Le Havre in June 1944 and there were many losses at sea. In early 1945 prior to the German surrender there was rather more success with the remaining S-Boats but only about fifteen were left in this theatre when the war ended. In the Mediterranean the final hunting ground of S-Boats was the Adriatic where they operated against the partisans of Yugoslavia and the clandestine sea traffic which supplied them.

The output of S-Boats was never spectacular since priority was given to other weapons of war, but in 1942 there were forty-one new boats; in 1943, thirty-eight; in 1944, sixty-four, and in 1945 there were fourteen. Many improvements were made to the original design and the illustration typifies the later type of boat, in this case the S-195 series of 1944. The S-26 series of 1940 introduced the idea of the faired in fore torpedo tubes and high forecastle. Subsequent boats all had this type of layout but there were increases in power and armament. To give superior protection against enemy ships – the British

built more motor gunboats to counter the S-Boats – there was a new type of bridge introduced in mid-1943, the 'Kalotte' bridge, an armoured casting of excellent ballistic design, rather like a tank turret in shape. This gave excellent protection to key control personnel and the steering and engine controls which were all susceptible to a hit taken on the old unarmoured bridges. Added gun armament was another feature and twin 2 cm guns aft and a single 2 cm gun in a forecastle 'well' were standard on this class. The engines were the later Daimler-Benz V-20 MB 501 diesels each of 2,000 hp, which became the standard S-Boat engines from 1940. These gave a top speed of up to 42 knots in this series.

The vessel is shown in the very pale grey which was chosen as the most effective standard colour for S-Boats, giving the most visual concealment at a distance in most conditions of light and weather. Tests carried out by the British Admiralty in 1945–46 with a captured S-Boat showed that the low silhouette and smooth contours gave minimum shadow – only the bow knuckle gave a shadow and this was obscured by the wash. In contrast a British MTB, with a very cluttered outline and high silhouette threw much shadow and could generally be spotted visually by an S-Boat before the MTB saw the S-Boat.

36. **Biber 90:** Midget Submarine, Germany

The German Kriegsmarine came very late to the idea of midget submarines, and they were considered only as a 'last ditch' device to cause maximum chaos to Allied naval forces in the North Sea and English Channel in the last year or so of the war. There had been only passing consideration of midget submarines when the U-Boat fleet was being planned in pre-war years, and priority was accorded to the big ocean going types needed to wage war against Allied shipping in the Atlantic. The British demonstrated what could be done with midget submarines when they attacked *Tirpitz* in 1943. With an invasion of Europe by the Allies appearing imminent, a new naval branch was set up to design, build, and operate midget submarines. Known as Kleinkampfverband (small weapon unit), this organisation was an independent command, not linked to U-Boat command.

Some very ingenious designs for small one-man units were quickly produced, and a number of them were selected for production and built in some numbers. The designs were mostly somewhat primitive, at least in so far as construction was concerned, for the boats had to be built when German industry was beset by disruption from Allied bombing and was short of materials and manpower. There were thus many breakdowns in operational craft and the finish and fitting left much to be desired. Of the designs accepted for production, the Seehund (Seal) or Type XXVII B was quite successful, being about as big as the 'human torpedoes' in size and carried another torpedo slung beneath it. The Marder (Marten) was of the same general type, with an underslung torpedo which was simply released from the craft when lined up with the target. Over 300 of each of these types was built. Both Seal and Marder types had electric motors only.

A much more seaworthy and elaborate type of craft was the Biber (Beaver), best known of all the German midget submarines, and generally similar to the Seehund. The Biber had a

146

single operator like the other midgets, and he sat in a midship conning compartment with a cupola fitted with armoured glass. Periscopes were provided and a small 12 hp gasoline engine gave a speed of 10 knots on the surface. An electric battery motor gave an underwater speed of 6 knots. The boat weighed 7 tons, was 29½ ft long, 3 ft 8 inches wide, and 5½ ft deep. It had a maximum range of up to 300 km, and could dive to 500 metres, being provided with ballast tanks. It was, in fact, a true submarine in miniature. About 325 Biber boats were built. The armament was two torpedoes, slung one each side in recesses below the hull and held and released magnetically.

The method of operation of these midget submarines was actually to sail under their own power from Dutch and Channel ports to carry out a mission. There was provision for towing to a suitable release point, either by a full-size submarine or a surface vessel, but shortage of ships in the 1944–45 period most often meant that the midget craft operated on their own. In view of the large numbers built, these German midget craft did not enjoy great success, as often as not due to mechanical break-down. Typical of defects which caused operations to be aborted was *Biber 90* captured by the British in December 1944, in which the crewman was found to be dead from carbon monoxide poisoning due to exhaust leaks while the boat was running on the surface. With the exception of the Seehund, the German midget submarines all had a one-man crew and this may well have affected operational results for there were exceptional psychological demands on a lone operator in the claustrophobic atmosphere of a small underwater craft. This actual vessel is now preserved in the Imperial War Museum, London.

37. **Hornet:** Aircraft Carrier, U.S.A.

The aircraft carrier *Hornet* was one of the best known of all U.S. Navy ships in World War 2 and she was one of the first of the long line of attack carriers which served the American fleet in the war years. Yet this famous ship lasted little over a year before being sunk in action. *Hornet* was one of a class of three, *Yorktown*, *Hornet*, and *Enterprise* which were the first big carriers for the U.S. Navy designed as such from the keel up. Prior to these ships, the U.S. Navy had *Langley*, a small converted collier and their first carriers, the big *Lexington* and *Saratoga*, converted from battle cruiser hulls, and the small *Ranger* which was the first actual carrier to be built, commissioned in 1934. From experience with *Ranger* it was decided by the Navy Board that something bigger was required, not less than 20,000 tons displacement. This led to the design of the 'Yorktown' class which were essentially no more than a lengthened version of *Ranger*. One big difference was that the new ships had the engine exhaust trunked into one big funnel in the 'island' superstructure, while the *Ranger* had small side exhausts which were less satisfactory.

Much careful thought went into the design and the new ships were quite revolutionary. The displacement was 19,800 tons standard, the length overall 809½ ft, and the beam was 83 ft, though the flight deck was 109½ ft at its widest point. The draught was 28 ft. The hull was fully armoured with a 3 inch armoured main deck – the hangar deck – and a 4 inch side armour belt and main bulkheads. The boiler rooms were amidships,

with four shaft geared turbines giving 120,000 shp; this gave the ship a top speed of 33 knots. Above the main deck, the flight deck was built as an unarmoured superstructure, the flight deck itself being wood planked.

The design philosophy has been the source of much subsequent argument. The contemporary new British carriers of the 'Illustrious' class had the flight deck armoured and was an integral part of the hull. While this gave superior protection it involved more building time and expense – and took longer to repair if damage was sustained. Nonetheless, the British carriers could sustain damage, even with an armoured flight deck, though the damage was usually more localised. The American practice of making the flight deck part of the superstructure greatly speeded building and repair time – important factors during the war years – but generally led to extensive damage by fire and blast when bombs were received on board. It was not until 1945 that new U.S. carriers with armoured flight decks appeared, all other war construction of carriers following the style of the 'Yorktown' class.

Yorktown and *Enterprise* were

the first two built, ordered under the 1933 estimates and commissioned in 1937 and 1938. Both won great fame in World War 2, and *Enterprise* was the only survivor of the class. *Hornet* was ordered in 1938 and was built by the Newport News Shipbuilding Co., Newport News, Virginia. Features of the ships included three aircraft lifts, two catapults in the forward end of the flight deck, and two catapults in the hangar deck which allowed aircraft to be launched out through the side of the ship through openings which could be shuttered when not required. These hangar deck catapults were not actually used. Arrestor wires, barriers, and windbreaks were fitted to the flight deck, and on each side of the ship just below flight deck level were the walkways and sponsons which also carried most of the ship's armament of eight 5 inch guns, sixteen 1·1 inch machine guns, and later twenty-three 20 mm Oerlikons.

Hornet was laid down in September 1939 and was launched little over a year later on 14 December 1940, her building greatly speeded by the war in Europe and America's need to re-arm quickly. The ship fitted out and commissioned in October 1941, her captain being Marc. E. Mitscher, an experienced naval pilot who went on to become one on the U.S. Navy's most famous admirals and exponents of aircraft carrier warfare. *Hornet* was still storing ship and completing trials when the Japanese attacked Pearl Harbor on 7 December 1941, but within three weeks the ship was sailing on her shakedown cruise with her air squadrons embarked.

Her very first operational cruise was both dramatic and historic. President Roosevelt wished to strike a defiant blow on Japan to retaliate in some degree for the humiliation of Pearl Harbor and to show the American people that they were striking back. The Naval Staff suggested flying Army bombers from a carrier to bomb Tokyo, and the project was found feasible so long as critical factors of fuel and payload were properly calculated. *Hornet* was available and trials were conducted off Norfolk, Virginia, in February 1942 with two North American B-25 Mitchell bombers, the type considered most suitable for the raid in terms of take-off ability from a short run, bomb load, and range. The result was that sixteen B-25 bombers with extra fuel tankage were embarked by crane for the cruise towards Japan to carry out this mission.

Commander of the squadron was Colonel James H. Doolittle. To maintain secrecy the aircraft were embarked from Alameda, San Francisco, so that *Hornet* could traverse the Panama Canal with her normal aircraft on board. On 2 April 1942, she headed for the Pacific as part of Task Force 16, formed for the mission. Escorting was her sister ship *Enterprise* with her normal naval aircraft on board, plus cruisers, destroyers and fleet oilers. After refuelling at sea the carriers made for a point 500 miles due east of Tokyo and the B-25 bombers were flown off. This was extremely hazardous – such big aircraft had not flown from carriers before – but all got safely airborne. The raid was extremely successful, though no more than a token assault, and the aircraft made their way on to China, as part of the plan since they could not land on *Hornet*. Though the planes were lost, most of the crews survived.

From this operation *Hornet* sailed back to Pearl Harbor, and in late May 1942 Task Force 16 sailed for the Midway Islands where a Japanese amphibious force was known to be heading.

The Battle of Midway was the first major sea battle carried out solely by opposing carrier aircraft, the surface fleets not meeting. Three Japanese carriers, including *Akagi*, were sunk in that battle. In June 1942 *Hornet* had a new captain and for the next four months she carried out various supporting missions in the Solomons and Guadalcanal. In October her aircraft carried out successful strikes at Bougainville and later that month her task force (now TF 17) sailed for the Santa Cruz islands to oppose a Japanese force heading for the area. On 26 October, *Hornet*'s aircraft were launched to attack the Japanese ships, but a simultaneous Japanese air attack caught *Hornet* undefended and early in the forenoon she was bombed and torpedoed. Major damage was done by a stricken Val torpedo bomber which was deliberately crashed into *Hornet*'s island, went through the unarmoured flight deck to the hangar below, and there its bomb-load exploded. Another aircraft also crashed into her and soon she was ablaze. Escorting ships took off the crew (over 100 were killed) and she was then shelled by U.S. ships to sink her and finally torpedoed by approaching Japanese destroyers –

the dramatic end to a short but eventful career.

38. **Illustrious**: Aircraft Carrier, U.K.

While *Hornet* represented U.S. Navy thinking on aircraft carriers at the start of World War 2, *Illustrious* typified the British ideas, which were in many ways different. At the time the 'Yorktown' class ships were being planned in U.S.A., the British naval staff were contemplating future requirements. One prototype carrier, the famous *Ark Royal*, was under construction, but the feeling at the Admiralty was that a fully armoured flight deck and hangar would be of prime importance in any future war, particularly in view of the strength of the German Luftwaffe. *Ark Royal* was not armoured in this way, and so the new design was actually a slightly smaller ship of the same displacement (23,000 tons), the size being reduced to compensate for the extra weight of the armour plate.

Illustrious was 745 ft overall, had a 94 ft beam, a draught of 25 ft, and triple geared shaft turbines of 110,000 hp giving a speed of 30 knots. The freeboard was 43 ft compared with $60\frac{1}{2}$ ft for the unarmoured *Ark Royal*. The armoured hangar (3 inch top, 4 inch sides, and 1 inch floor) was virtually a box pierced only by the lifts at each end, but armoured shutters were supplied to seal the ends of the box – though later these were replaced by asbestos curtains. There was $4\frac{1}{2}$ inches of side armour at the waterline and light armour on the bridge. The ship was laid down in April 1937 and launched two years later in April 1939. She was completed in April/May 1940. After a shake-down cruise to Bermuda the ship had a refit to overcome final problems, and complete degaussing, and the catapult and landing gear were fitted.

Illustrious was the first British carrier to operate with a system of arrestor wires and crash barriers. The wire mesh barriers protected aircraft parked forward from any aircraft which missed the arrestor wires. This greatly speeded landing operations, since prior to barriers each newly landed aircraft had to be struck down the forward lift to leave a clear deck for the following aircraft – this took several minutes. With the barrier system, each aircraft on landing was released from the arrestor wire and then taxied forward over the barrier, which was lowered for the purpose. While the aircraft was parked forward the barrier was re-positioned for the next aircraft to land; the landing interval was reduced to well under a minute with a well-trained flight deck crew. The barrier system was subsequently used in all British and American aircraft carriers until the angled deck system was introduced in the later 1950s.

In August 1940 *Illustrious* joined the Mediterranean fleet where there was now much naval activity due to the Italian declaration of war in June 1940. The first sortie, a raid on an airfield at Calato was flown early in September. Two weeks later there was a much bigger raid on Benghazi harbour where merchant ships and an Italian destroyer were sunk and the harbour entrances were mined. At the end of September and in October there were operations in support of Malta convoys. In October there were operations in connection with the landings in Crete by British forces. On 11/12 November 1940 came the raid on the Italian Battle Fleet at Taranto which was at the time a sensational feat of arms for a hard-pressed Britain. It also fore-shadowed the even more successful Japanese attack on Pearl Harbor just over a year later. In the Taranto raid *Illustrious* launched twenty-one Swordfish aircraft for a night raid which sank one battleship, severely disabled two more, and damaged others as well as destroying some harbour facilities.

Operations in the next two months included sorties against Bardice and Tripoli and strikes in the Aegean area, as well as Malta convoy support. In the New Year of 1941 *Illustrious* formed part of the escort screen for a fast convoy from the Malta area to Alexandria with urgent military supplies. The success of British carriers in the Mediterranean – particularly *Illustrious* – had caused the Germans to move a special anti-shipping air unit to Trapani, intended to counter British carrier power. *Illustrious* had a Fulmar reconnaissance fighter squadron embarked which was scrambled to counter a threatened torpedo attack at low level by Italian Sparviero bombers. This distracted Ju 87 Stukas from the German special group from a high level dive bombing attack. Six bombs hit *Illustrious*, one of them blowing out the after lift and another penetrating the flight deck ahead of the lift and exploding in the hangar. The ship's steering was put out of action and she had to steer by engines only. The remaining damage was superficial. Most important, however, was that the armoured flight deck concept was fully vindicated by the relatively light damage sustained from a bombing raid of such intensity.

The ship returned to Malta, burning from the attack, and surviving near-misses from more dive-bombing attacks. *Illustrious* was berthed for repairs and suffered yet more bombing attacks while in dock for repair to the steering. It was evident that more extensive repairs would have to be carried out away from the threat of air attack. The U.S. Navy's Norfolk Navy Yard was contracted for the work. In late January *Illustrious* sailed for Alexandria and made passage to Norfolk, Virginia, via the Suez Canal, Indian Ocean and Durban. As the after end of the ship needed considerable rebuilding, the deck and stern were lengthened by about 50 ft. The AA armament was amended so that ten 20 mm Oerlikons were added to the sixteen 4·5 inch high angle guns (eight twin turrets) and forty-eight 2 pdr pom-poms

which formed the original armament.

In December 1941, *Illustrious* returned to Britain. In March 1942, the ship sailed for South Africa where she was to support the landings at Diego Suarez to capture Madagascar which was held by the Vichy French. Wide ranging operations in the Indian Ocean with the British Eastern Fleet took up the remainder of the year and included activity around Ceylon. Returning to Britain in January 1943, the ship had a six month refit, which included a further lengthening of the flight deck, new twin Oerlikon mounts, new radar, and extra arrestor wires.

In July 1943 *Illustrious* was back on active service and she made one operational cruise with the battleship H.M.S. *Anson* and U.S.S. *Alabama* in a feinted attack on Norway. She then went to Gibraltar and became part of the famous Force H to cover the landings at Salerno in September 1943. This proved fairly uneventful, for the Italian fleet surrendered and there was only limited Luftwaffe action. *Illustrious* returned to England and was prepared for service in the Far East again where she was to operate some of the 'new generation' of modern (mostly

American) aircraft then entering service. By February 1944 she was back in the Indian Ocean and was soon involved in an unsuccessful search for a Japanese cruiser force which made a brief appearance. Next came a major operation when *Illustrious* joined with U.S.S. *Saratoga* for a raid on the Japanese base at Sabang, Sumatra. Next her aircraft attacked oil refineries at Surabaya in Java, and this was followed by a foray in the Andaman Islands as a diversion from the main U.S. fleet attack on the Marianas, in June 1944. In the next month, July, came a much bigger air attack on Sabang, with two other carriers joining *Illustrious*, and a bombardment by battleships.

In the next three months there was a refit at Durban, South Africa. In December 1944 there were no less than four fleet carriers in the East Indies and *Illustrious* with *Indomitable* flew strikes against oil refineries at Palembang in December 1944. A month later all four carriers in the fleet flew strikes against the Sumatra refineries with colossal effect. The carriers now all joined the British Pacific Fleet (Task Force 57) and there *Illustrious* took part in air strikes in conjunction with the Okinawa land-

ings and against Formosa. In April 1945 *Illustrious* survived a Kamikaze (suicide plane) attack, the ship's AA armament diverting the path of the aircraft which exploded in the sea alongside the ship. This caused strain to the hull, with some cracked frames, and she returned to Britain for a refit which lasted until the end of the war and beyond.

Illustrious's long and arduous war service was over, and she served the Royal Navy as a trials and training carrier for another nine years until 1954. Over the years her successive refits changed her appearance considerably, and she ended the war rather different to her 1940 guise. By 1945 she had become 748½ ft overall, and the flight deck had been stretched from 620 ft to 740 ft; the full load displacement had increased to 31,630 tons and the complement (because of armament and aircraft changes) had increased from about 1,230 to 1,997. The gun armament in 1945 was sixteen 4·5 inch guns, forty 2 pdr (in five, eight barrelled mounts), fifty-two 20 mm Oerlikons (in single and twin mounts) and three 40 mm Bofors guns.

Illustrious had two equally famous sister ships, *Victorious* and *Formidable*, and a fourth sister, *Indomitable*, which was altered while being built so as to have thinner side armour but an extra half-length hangar. Two late sister ships, *Implacable* and *Indefatigable*, were also built to this standard. All the ships had distinguished war histories.

The ship is shown in the Admiralty Medium Disruptive camouflage scheme in 1942.

39/40. **Furious: Glorious:** Aircraft Carriers, U.K.

Furious was one of the great veteran ships of World War 2, already old when war broke out, and indeed, a relic of the World War 1. When built, *Furious*, with her sisters *Courageous* and *Glorious*, was a large 19,000 ton 'light' battle-cruiser. The construction of these ships was forced ahead by Lord Fisher in 1915–17, with characteristics which included huge 18 inch guns and a speed of nearly 32 knots. An early decision was made to remove the forward 18 inch turret so that seaplanes could be carried. In 1917–18 she was fitted with a flying-off deck, then a landing deck aft. By the end of World War 1 she was one of Britain's few early aircraft carriers with a successful record.

At this time she was still fitted with the original battle-cruiser superstructure which limited the aircraft operating potential, and in the 1922–25 period she was completely reconstructed as a flat top aircraft carrier with lifts to a hangar under the flight deck. A retractable navigation bridge was fitted at the forward end of the flight deck, and small navigating positions were built into the corners of the flight deck (linked below the deck) for use when the navigating bridge was retracted, or for manoeuvring in harbour. In the original concept there were two hangars below the flight deck, and doors at the front end of the hangar opened out on to a foredeck from which aircraft could theoretically be launched straight from the upper hangar. The rebuilt ship was now radically different from the original battle-cruiser appearance and proved to be very successful in service. This resulted in her sister ships *Courageous* and *Glorious* being similarly converted in the late 1920s.

In the 1937–39 period *Furious* was gradually modernised. By the time the war started, she had had her armament changed to the latest twin 4 inch high angle gun mounts, six in all, and four eight-barrelled 2 pdr 'pom-pom' mounts, giving a much superior anti-aircraft armament. In conjunction with the new guns a low 'island' superstructure was built on the starboard side of the flight deck. This carried the high angle directors and the gun control position, though navigating and flying control were still restricted to the forward positions. The original facility for flying off from the hangar deck was discarded, the extra forward deck space being used for some of the gun mounts. When war broke out *Furious* was engaged as a training carrier for new pilots, but she was soon withdrawn and joined the Home Fleet where she was involved in some search operations for German surface raiders and then acted as screen for some Atlantic convoys. With the German invasion of Norway, in April 1940, *Furious* steamed to Narvik where she supported the battleship *Warspite* and her destroyer screen in the famous Battle of Narvik. *Furious* flew air cover for this operation and then supported land operations on the mainland. With her sister ship *Glorious*, she ferried R.A.F. aircraft to and from Norway and covered the withdrawal, *Glorious* being sunk in these operations.

In June 1940 *Furious* carried a large consignment of Bank of England gold bullion to Canada for safe keeping. She continued to operate in Northern waters, acted as an aircraft ferry to West Africa and Gibraltar, and, in July 1941 she sailed with *Victorious* to fly off an attack on Petsamo to support hard-pressed Russian forces. In September 1941 she took Spitfires to Malta, and after a refit in U.S.A., she joined Force H at Gibraltar and escorted one of the biggest Malta convoys, in 'Operation Pedestal', August 1942, when Malta was resupplied against heavy air and sea attack. *Furious* took part in 'Operation Torch', the landings in North Africa, flying air cover. Back with the Home Fleet the ship covered Russian convoys, then joined the carrier force which mounted an attack by Barracuda torpedo bombers against the big German battleship *Tirpitz* in Kaa Fjord, Norway, in April 1944. This was a most successful operation which disabled the target ship. Further operations in Norwegian waters followed, but in September 1944 she was laid up, being now one of the oldest carriers in the fleet. By this time there were very many new carriers in service and *Furious* could be dispensed with after her years of hard and continous service.

In 1944 *Furious* displaced 22,450 tons, was 786¼ ft long, 89¾ ft in beam, 26 ft in draught and had a flight deck 107 ft at its widest and 576 ft long. There was 3 inches of side armour and 1/3 inches of deck armour. Four shaft geared turbines gave 90,895 shp with a speed of 28½ knots. The complement was about 1,300 officers and men.

Furious is shown as in early 1941, in plain dark grey. The black section aft was to mask stain from the funnel exhaust.

41. **Schleswig-Holstein:** Battleship, Germany

The battleship *Schleswig-Holstein* was one of the oldest large warships to remain in commission with any of the major navies of World War 2. Though rated as a battleship she was actually a 'pre-dreadnought', in that she was one of the last major battleships to be built before the British *Dreadnought* appeared and started off a new era of battleship design. *Schleswig-Holstein* was a typical early twentieth-century battleship with her four 11 inch guns disposed in a twin turret fore and aft and

secondary armament one of fourteen 6·7 inch guns in broadside barbettes. She was actually commissioned in 1905, the year the British *Dreadnought* was launched. Subsequent German battleships were all 'dreadnoughts'. At the end of World War 1 with much of the old Imperial German Navy fleet either scuttled, sunk, or surrendered as reparations, the terms of the Versailles Treaty allowed Germany to retain certain obsolete units as training ships. Among these were *Schleswig-Holstein* and her sister ships *Schlesien* and *Hannover*.

These ships were already veritable museum pieces – overtaken by the march of time – in 1914, and in the inter-war period they were considered by the Allied powers to be valueless other than for sea training of personnel, and possibly coast defences. The displacement of this class was 13,200 tons standard, and they were 419 ft long, 72 ft in beam, and drew 26½ ft. Three shaft reciprocating engines of 16,000 hp gave a top speed when new of 18 knots. They were designed to be either coal or oil fired. These ships took part in the Battle of Jutland in 1916, and a sister ship *Pommern* was sunk in that action.

In post-war years the three survivors (another, *Deutschland* was scrapped), were all altered slightly, one major change being the trunking of the two forward funnels into one thicker one to carry fumes and smoke clear of the spotting top. The secondary armament was altered to ten 5·9 inch guns. *Hannover* was converted to a disarmed radio-controlled target ship in 1935, and spent the war as an accommodation ship. *Schleswig-Holstein* and *Schlesien* saw considerable service, however, and were, in fact, included in the Naval Staff war plans, being earmarked for operations in the Baltic where the potential enemies, Poland and Russia, did not offer too great a naval threat.

It fell to *Schleswig-Holstein* to fire the first shots by a warship in World War 2 when she and *Schlesien* engaged forts at Hela and Westerplatte. *Schleswig-Holstein*'s objective, much the most important, was the destruction of the Westerplatte fort which guarded the entrance to Danzig harbour. At a few minutes after 0440 hours on the morning of 1 September 1939, *Schleswig-Holstein* opened fire on the fort with her 11 inch and 5·9 inch guns at a range of only a few hundred metres, virtually point blank. At first light a small landing force was put ashore, but was repulsed by the Poles. The battleship then remained on station firing at the fort for six days until it was reduced to rubble and the garrison surrendered. *Schleswig-Holstein*'s action was the most notable in a campaign in which the naval action consisted of little more than blockading the coast and and ports of Poland and attempting – with some success and some failures – to prevent the few ships of the Polish Navy escaping to fight on in the Allied cause.

Both the veteran battleships served in the Baltic throughout World War 2, almost solely in the role of fire support ships to the army ashore. *Schlesien* was eventually sunk by a mine on 4 May 1945, off Swinemunde and rested on the sea bed until about 1950 when she was raised and scrapped. *Schleswig-Holstein* was bombed and holed by Russian aircraft at Gdynia on 21 March 1945, where she sank in very shallow water with her guns and superstructure intact. There she continued to give fire support to the army until the area was over-run by the Soviets. This was not quite the end of the story for *Schleswig-Holstein* was handed over to the Russians as a war reparation at the Allied Berlin Conference in 1945 – along with a number of other German ships. However, she was scrapped in the 1950–56 period.

Schleswig-Holstein was built at Kiel by the firm of Germania-werft. In World War 2 her AA armament of twenty 3·4 inch guns was replaced or augmented by various 20 mm and 37 mm AA guns of modern type. The illustration shows the ship as she appeared in dazzle camouflage in the latter part of World War 2.

42. **Alabama:** Battleship, U.S.A.

After World War 1 there was a 'holiday' in capital ship construction which affected all the great powers. Partly due to the world economic recession, the United States was later than other nations in building new capital ships, even under the limitations of the Washington Treaty. It was in 1934 that Congress voted funds for building two new battleships, but it was not until 1936 that final approval for construction was given, and the two ships concerned, *North Carolina* and *Washington*, both of 35,000 tons displacement and with a main battery of nine

16 inch guns, were completed in 1941 just before U.S.A. entered World War 2. In May 1938, Congress authorised four more new battleships of the same type. The original project for these vessels was known as 'Battleship 1939'.

As a result of study of the original *North Carolina* design and contemporary foreign ships, it was decided to alter the new ships slightly to give an 18 inch armour belt rather than the 16 inch belt of the *North Carolina* and *Washington*. To keep within the limitations of the Washington Treaty, 35,000 tons for a battleship, it was necessary to compensate for the increased armour weight by building a shorter more compact ship. Hence the four new battleships were given a single trunked funnel (rather than the two funnels of the original design), the superstructure was grouped more tightly in a pyramid amidships, and the hull armour belt was flanked outboard by tanks which could hold fuel oil or water ballast (or could be kept empty) so that a torpedo would pierce these tanks before reaching the armour belt. This gave the hull sides a 'step'. The four new ships, in order of building, were *South Dakota, Indiana, Massachusetts,* and *Alabama* (hull numbers BB.57 to BB.60). The keel of *Alabama* was laid on 1 February 1940, by which time Britain and France were at war with Germany. *Alabama* was built at Norfolk Navy Yard, Va, and was launched by Mrs Lister Hill, wife of Senator Hill of Alabama, on 16 February 1942. By this time, of course, the United States was at war and had suffered the Pearl Harbor catastrophe when most of the old battleships had been sunk or damaged. With a big priority programme, *Alabama* was fitted out in only six months and commissioned on 16 August 1942. She left Norfolk Yavy Yard in November of that year for a 'shake-down' cruise in Chesapeake Bay.

The illustration shows *Alabama* as she appeared in November 1942, painted in the impressive colour scheme known as MEASURE 12, an early three tone graded scheme intended to make the ship difficult to distinguish from a distance. The lower hull colour, navy blue, applied in an irregular pattern, merged well with the sea; the upper hull was ocean grey, and the superstructure was in a streaky pattern of ocean grey merged into a light shade known as haze grey intended to blend well with an overcast sky. This colour scheme was used extensively in the first year of hostilities (1942) on U.S. warships but it was discarded by the end of 1942 since experience at early major battles showed that pattern painted ships actually showed up better than those in plain colours. *Alabama* was one of the last ships painted in MEASURE 12 pattern.

Alabama gave distinguished war service. From May–August she was with Task Force 61, the Navy element serving with the British Home Fleet and covering Russian convoys. In September 1943 she moved to the Pacific and in the closing months of the year was one of the battleship force giving gunfire support to the Gilbert and Nauru Island landings. In February 1944, in Task Force 58, she bombarded Kwajalein Atoll and Namur during the invasion of the Marshall Islands. For the rest of 1944 *Alabama* was involved in nearly all the naval operations concerned with the 'island hopping' campaigns in the Pacific, including the great Marianas 'Turkey Shoot'. *Alabama*, with a long range air-warning radar installation by then, was the first ship to detect the approaching Japanese aircraft on that occasion. In the early part of 1945, *Ala-*

bama was back in the U.S.A. for refit and returned to active service in the Pacific for the Okinawa actions of May/June 1945. This was the time of both Kamikaze aircraft attacks in huge numbers and a violent typhoon which crippled many U.S. ships, but *Alabama* survived all this unscathed, accounting for two enemy aircraft. In the last month of the war, *Alabama* was among the battleship force bombarding the Japanese mainland. She returned to the U.S.A. in October 1945 and in 1946 was refitted and placed in 'mothballs' in the reserve fleet. Stricken from the U.S.N. in 1962, she was purchased by the State of Alabama in 1964 and is now a state memorial, open to visitors, at Mobile, Alabama.

Alabama (details as completed, 1942). Displacement: 35,000 tons, 44,500 tons (full load). Length overall: 679½ ft. Length at waterline: 666 ft. Beam (max): 108 ft 1½ inches. Draught (max): 36 ft 2 inches. Armament: nine 16 inch Cal 0·45, Mk 6 (in three turrets); twenty 5 inch Cal 0·38, Mk 12 (in ten twin turrets); twenty-four 40 mm Cal 0·56 (in twin mounts); twenty-two 20 mm Cal 0·70 (in single mounts); three seaplanes with two catapults. Armour: 16–

18 inches maximum. Machinery: Eight Foster-Wheeler boilers, four shaft-geared turbines, giving 130,000 shp, maximum speed 28 knots. Complement: 2,332 officers and men.

43. **Prince of Wales:** Battleship, U.K.

Aside from the battleships *Nelson* and *Rodney*, and the completion of the war-programme battle-cruisers *Hood, Renown,* and *Repulse,* Great Britain added no new capital ships to her fleet between the two world wars. This 'holiday' in the building of capital ships was due to several factors, among them the economic depression of the period, the belief that there would be no more wars, and the various treaties – notably the Washington and London Naval Treaties – intended to limit the armaments of the major powers. There was clearly a need to supplement the battleships of the 'Queen Elizabeth' and 'Royal Sovereign' classes, however, which dated from 1915, and in 1934 preliminary work commenced on the design of a new class of battleship.

Under the treaty terms, standard displacement was limited

to 35,000 tons and main gun calibre to 16 inches, though a further treaty in 1935 imposed a new gun limitation of 14 inches. The other nations participating in the original Washington Treaty (France, Italy, Japan, U.S.A.) largely ignored this new condition, but the British honoured the 14 inch rule and incorporated main guns of this calibre into the new design. This caused considerable problems for, in order to make up for the lower calibre gun, it was decided to mount quadruple turrets – three of them – giving a broadside of twelve 14 inch guns altogether. A completely new type of gun and turret had to be designed – in itself an immense and complicated task – but it was further discovered that the superimposed forward turret ('B' turret) would cause stability problems due to the weight of the gun mountings and the desired amount of armour protection. Thus 'B' turret was reduced to a twin mount in the design stage and the main armament was finalised at ten 14 inch guns.

Two ships were ordered to the new design under the 1936 naval estimates, named *King George V* (in honour of the king who died that year) and *Prince of Wales*. Three more ships, *Duke of York*, *Anson*, and *Howe*, were ordered under the 1937 naval estimates, by which time the threat of possible European war with Germany was already apparent and Britain was beginning an urgent rearmament programme.

Apart from the unusual main armament, the layout of the 'King George V' class ships was well-balanced. In particular there was a good appreciation of the anti-aircraft problem which was at the time of the design work untested by war. The threat of air attack on large fleet units was only too apparent, however, and the events of World War 2 were to prove that the battleship was extremely vulnerable to such attack, even with the most sophisticated AA guns and defence measures. In the 'King George V' class ships there were sixteen 5·25 inch high angle dual purpose guns (for AA and surface fire) in eight turrets, disposed four each side amidships. There were four eight-barrel 2 pdr (40 mm) 'pom-poms' (popularly called 'Chicago Pianos') and provision for four quadruple 0·5 inch Vickers machine gun mounts. By the time the ships commissioned for service, however, the war was already in progress; the 0·5 inch machine guns had proven to be virtually useless in service and so were not mounted. Instead the various ships of the class were given extra pom-poms and 20 mm Oerlikon mounts of either the single or twin type. *King George V* and *Prince of Wales* carried rocket launchers, for Unrotated Projectiles (UP) when they were first commissioned, but these also proved unsatisfactory in service and were removed very quickly. The associated armour protection on these 'King George V' class ships was among the best of its time for a ship of the size, in some ways better than the arrangements on the biggest German battleships, *Bismarck* and *Tirpitz*. There was some 12,500 tons of armour plate including 6 inches horizontally at deck level and 15 inches vertically alongside the magazines. There was a very elaborate watertight subdivision below decks, including a 2 inch thick torpedo belt.

Prince of Wales herself was laid down at the Cammell Laird yard, Birkenhead, on 1 January 1937 and was launched on 21 February 1939, by which time it seemed inevitable that Britain might soon be at war with Germany. Due to the urgency of the situation construction proceeded at great pace. *King George V*,

which was laid down and launched at the same time by Vickers-Armstrong was actually finished first, in October 1940. *Prince of Wales* commissioned on 31 March 1941, and such was the speed of events that workmen from the yard were still on board when the ship joined the fleet. The complex quadruple turrets gave particular trouble, and this affected the performance of the ship during her first action when she was engaged with other ships of the British Home Fleet in the action against the great German battleship *Bismarck*.

Prince of Wales became involved in this action on 24 May 1941. She was still virtually a new untried ship, with her crew not fully familiar with the equipment and still suffering from the inevitable 'teething troubles' of a new ship. *Prince of Wales* was in company with the battlecruiser *Hood*, converging on *Bismarck* at 0600 hours, and closing the range. The action was short and sharp and resulted in the sensational and unexpected sinking of *Hood* which literally blew up soon after being hit by *Bismarck*'s escorting cruiser *Prinz Eugen*. Meanwhile *Prince of Wales* had straddled *Bismarck* but was unable to fire full salvoes mainly due to defects in the turrets. Shells from both the German ships now hit *Prince of Wales*, one passing through the bridge structure and killing or wounding most of the personnel in this position. Other shots hit a gun director and the ship's aircraft, but two shells which penetrated the ship's side failed to explode, which was fortunate for one of them entered a shell room. About 400 tons of flood water came on board as a result of the damage and *Prince of Wales* was forced to break off the action, giving *Bismarck* a temporary respite in the chase.

After repairs *Prince of Wales* was soon back in the news, for in August 1941 she took on board a most important passenger, the British Prime Minister Winston Churchill, for his first historic meeting with President Roosevelt at Argentia, Newfoundland, which resulted in the signing of the Atlantic Charter ensuring Anglo-American co-operation for the duration of the war.

By now there was a new threat to Britain in the Far East where it was seen that Japanese forces could attack the British possessions of Malaya and Singapore. A new British Far Eastern Fleet was set up, with Admiral Sir Tom Phillips as C.-in-C. *Prince of Wales* became the flagship and

sailed from the River Clyde on 25 October 1941, arriving at Singapore on 2 December. A few days later, on 7 December 1941, came the Japanese attack on Pearl Harbor and a simultaneous invasion of Malaya. Admiral Phillips quickly organised a squadron to sail from Singapore to the Gulf of Siam in the hope of deterring the Japanese naval forces covering the invasion and supply fleet. Known as Force Z, the squadron consisted of the *Prince of Wales*, the old and inadequately armed battle-cruiser *Repulse*, and a screen of four destroyers. What was lacking, however, was the important element of air cover, for the few British Buffalo fighters available were needed to protect Singapore and lacked the range in any case. There was optimism on the British side that the squally weather and low clouds might deter air attacks, while *Prince of Wales*'s anti-aircraft armament was considered quite formidable. Force Z eventually turned south, heading back towards Singapore, but Japanese submarines and reconnaissance aircraft had been keeping track of the movements. One sortie by the Japanese 22nd Air Flotilla, flying from south Indo-China, turned back from an attempted night attack on the ships due to bad weather on 9 December. Next morning, however, at 1115 hours on 10 December, thirty-four bombers and fifty-one torpedo bombers of this same air flotilla swooped in on the ships from several directions. Torpedoes blew off the propellers of *Prince of Wales* and she was immobilised, a sitting target for repeated torpedo attacks. The more lightly armoured *Repulse* was first to sink, but within two hours of the start of the attack the battered *Prince of Wales* also sank and Britain's naval presence in those waters was virtually eliminated.

This was a stunning blow for Britain at a time when her fortunes were at a low ebb. Prime Minister Churchill heard the news of the sinking and recorded 'In all the war I never received a more direct shock'. So ended the short but eventful career of one of Britain's most prestigious battleships. Like the attack on Pearl Harbor a few days earlier, and the British attack on the Italian Fleet at Taranto, the immense vulnerability of the battleship to air attack was effectively demonstrated by the loss of the *Prince of Wales* and *Repulse*. From then on the aircraft carrier and her aircraft became dominant surface weapons of the offensive war at sea.

Displacement: 35,000 tons (nominal), 35,990 tons (actual), 39,460 tons (full load). Dimensions: 745 ft (overall), 700 ft (between perpendiculars), 103 ft (beam), $34\frac{1}{2}$ ft (mean maximum draught). Armament: ten 14 inch Mk VII guns (four × two turrets, two × one turret); forty-eight (six × eight) 2 pdr pom-poms; seven 20 mm, one 40 mm, sixteen (two × eight turrets); 5·25 inch Mk I gun. Armour: 15 inch maximum (sides), 6 inch maximum (deck). Propulsion: four shaft geared turbines giving 11,000 shp, eight 3-drum boilers. Maximum speed: 28·5 knots. Range: 14,000 miles at 10 knots. Fuel capacity: 3,700 tons. Aircraft: Two Walrus and catapult amidships. Complement: 1,640 officers and men (approx.).

44. **Altmark:** Supply Ship, Germany

The German Navy (Kriegsmarine) that was being built up in the 1930s faced some problems of deployment which were caused by Germany's geographical position and her post-1918 status. Whereas almost all the other major naval powers –

especially Britain, U.S.A., and France – had many overseas bases which could support warships with stores and fuel, much of Germany's territorial waters were in the Baltic and she had no overseas bases. While the idea of replenishment ships for the fleet was not new – all navies had colliers, oilers, and store ships of sorts – Germany's intended war policy of threatening enemy (i.e., British and French) commerce routes with capital ships could only be carried out if the commerce raiders themselves were able to stay on station or cruise at will without the continual need to return to German waters to re-store.

The only answer to this was to have large fast replenishment ships able to carry all the fuel and stores that a capital ship or large cruiser would need, and able to rendezvous in mid-ocean to carry out the transfer. With the view to supporting the new 'pocket battleships' of the 'Graf Spee' class in particular, four very large supply ships were included in the 1937 German Navy Estimates. They were *Altmark, Ermland, Dithmarschen,* and *Westerwald*. They all looked like contemporary motor tankers, though the after superstructure, in particular, was large

enough to indicate that they were more than just tankers.

The displacement was 10,847 tons standard and 22,500 tons fully laden. The overall length was 582 ft, the beam $72\frac{1}{2}$ ft and the deep load draft was $30\frac{1}{4}$ ft. *Altmark* was powered by four MAN diesel motors of 21,400 hp giving a speed of 21 knots. Her sisters had twin geared shaft turbines, however, giving similar power and top speed. The most lavish and extensive internal layout allowed 10,000 tons of oil fuel, 300 tons of lubricating oil, aviation fuel, water, and other liquid stores to be carried in the appropriate tankage. Solid stores included machinery spares, and clothing, while victualling stores of all kinds were carried. There were refrigeration rooms aft for perishable foods. Heavy calibre ammunition for re-supplying battleships was carried right forward in specially fitted shell rooms, with lifts to bring shells up on deck for transfer. Spare torpedoes were similarly carried. There was a large sick bay with medical staff and the ships were built to a very high standard of quality.

All four ships were completed in 1939 but no official mention of their building was ever made, and there was none of the usual celebration at launching and commissioning for the very good reason that the Kriegsmarine wished to keep their existence secret. For one significant reason, the ships were all armed, with the guns in concealed mounts which did not show outboard. The original armament, in fact, was three 15 cm guns, two 2 cm AA guns, and assorted machine guns. There was one 15 cm gun below each bridge wing behind false superstructure plates, which hinged away to reveal the gun. A similar arrangement was provided aft for a 15 cm gun on the centreline. The design of the ship took account of the guns and the decks were suitably stressed.

Under the war plans of the Kriegsmarine the four big supply ships were to take up ocean stations before any hostilities commenced, keep to a general area, and have the surface raiders rendezvous with them at suitable times so that they could replenish. *Altmark* was to support *Graf Spee* and left Germany for her supply station in the South Atlantic in early August 1939. *Graf Spee* herself left later, but before the Germans invaded Poland and so *ipso facto* triggered off the war. *Altmark* picked up a cargo of fuel oil in U.S.A., ostensibly to take back

to Germany. Once at sea, *Altmark* repainted her funnel pale yellow and changed the name on her bows and stern to *Sogne* of Oslo, flying, of course, the Norwegian flag. On 1 September 1939, she rendezvoused with *Graf Spee* and carried out refuelling of the small battleship by means of a hose passed astern. Several other meetings were arranged throughout September, *Altmark* passing to *Graf Spee* all the fuel and stores she could accommodate on board. *Graf Spee* then left *Altmark* in the middle of the South Atlantic and went off on a successful search for British merchant ships off the African coast.

In mid-October, *Graf Spee* and a captured prize ship rendezvoused with *Altmark* and 150 prisoners taken from the sunken merchant ships were transferred to the supply ship, as were some captured stores. A British merchant ship, *Trevanion*, which was captured and sunk by *Graf Spee* on 22 October managed to transmit the position by radio to Britain. This caused *Graf Spee* to clear the African coast, send *Altmark* south, and pass round the Cape. A ship was sunk off the South-East African coast (*Africa Star*) and the crew were allowed to escape ashore – except for the captain – thus establishing knowledge of *Graf Spee*'s presence in the area. The battleship made a rapid departure from the area, however, and again met *Altmark* in the South Atlantic, late in November. Two more ships fell victim to *Graf Spee*, one near St. Helena, and the battleship now decided to head for the South American coast. By this time 229 captured British seamen had been placed aboard *Altmark*. On 6 December 1939, there was another refuelling operation. Within a week *Graf Spee* had been trapped by the Royal Navy off the River Plate. *Graf Spee* scuttled herself on 16 December 1939, and *Altmark* was now ordered by radio to return to Germany, keeping radio silence. After keeping well south to repair her engines and celebrate Christmas, *Altmark* eventually set off for Germany on 21 January 1940. With great luck *Altmark* managed to evade all British ships seeking her, carrying yet another merchant ship name and now being painted grey. On 13 February 1940, *Altmark* reached Norwegian waters via the Faroes, and off Kristiansund and again off Bergen was challenged by Norwegian gunboats, which were unable to prevent her passage south.

The Royal Navy now knew of *Altmark*'s whereabouts and the cruiser *Arethusa* spotted her following an aircraft sighting. The destroyer *Cossack* now made for the ship, which steamed into Jossing Fjord on the south-west tip of Norway. The *Cossack* was ordered by the British Admiralty to intercept *Altmark* and rescue the prisoners believed to be aboard. Though Norway was still a neutral country the drama was acted out on the night of 16 February. *Cossack* followed *Altmark* into the fjord, secured alongside, put a boarding party on the *Altmark* and released the prisoners after a short but spirited fight with *Altmark*'s crew. The cry 'The Navy's Here' when *Cossack*'s crew arrived became one of the classic phrases of World War 2. The incident became one of the most famous in Royal Navy history, but it also caused diplomatic embarrassment because of Norway's neutrality.

After this episode *Altmark* lost much of her importance. She was renamed *Uckermark* as soon as she returned to Germany for a refit. The German surface raiders also found themselves greatly hampered in operating potential over the years ahead as the Royal Navy hunted the replenishment ships down. *Uckermark* had an inglorious end when she blew up while loading oil at Yokohama, Japan, in November 1942. *Altmark*'s sister ships all had eventful careers. *Ermland* was sunk in 1944, *Westerwald* was renamed *Nordmark* and was later inducted into the Royal Navy as *Bulawayo*, and *Dithmarschen* became the U.S. Navy's *Conecuh* after World War 2. These ships were the forerunners of what was to become a common type employed in post-war years by the major sea powers – the fast fleet replenishment ship – and *Nordmark* in post-war British hands was used, in fact, to develop many of the replenishment techniques subsequently used in the Royal Navy.

45. Java: Light Cruiser, Netherlands

The light cruiser *Java* was designed during World War 1 and was a large ship for her armament mainly because she was intended to be suitable for colonial use with an adequate range for service in the Dutch East Indies. Her sister ship was *Sumatra* and both were built in the early 1920s, *Java* by the Netherlands Dock Co. at Amsterdam. Launched in August 1921, she was first commissioned in 1925. In 1935 both ships completed refits which included the fitting of a distinctive tubular foremast and bridge structure similar to the style used in the German cruiser *Köln*. An aircraft catapult was fitted athwartships between the funnels, and two derricks were provided to handle floatplanes. As refitted the ships were 509½ ft long overall, 52½ ft in beam, and drew 18 ft. The standard displacement was 6,670 tons. Three shaft geared turbines gave 72,000 shp, and a top speed of 31 knots. The range was 4,800 miles at 12 knots. Main armament was ten 5·9 inch guns in single open mounts, four on the centre line and three each side. *Java* had eight 40 mm AA guns, and *Sumatra* had six. Rails and chutes aft allowed for twelve mines, and there were also saluting guns and light machine guns. Armour protection was fairly light, 2–3 inches on the side belt, 1 inch on deck, 4 inches on gun shields, and 5 inches on the conning tower.

When the Japanese struck in the East in December 1941, *Java* and a slightly larger semi-sister ship *De Ruyter* were the main units of the Dutch East Indies Fleet. In January 1942, the joint command of A.B.D.A. was set up, with Admiral Karel Doorman of the Royal Netherlands Navy as the naval commander, his flagship being *De Ruyter*. Japanese Navy task forces, escorting landing forces, were penetrating into the East Indies coming as far as Timor in a rapid progression. The A.B.D.A. command ships were based at Surabaya and Karel Doorman mustered all available Allied ships to attack the latest and largest Japanese task fleets approaching Borneo. Then followed the Battle of the Java Sea which was one of the blackest but most gallant episodes from the Allied point of view, for nearly all the Allied ships were sunk, in a fast running battle. Fate had also decreed that the Allied ships had no floatplanes aboard to act as spotters, for Doorman had had them disembarked at Surabaya in the belief that all the action would be at night. However, the Japanese forces were encountered sooner than expected, at about 1600 hours. Despite fierce gunfire, the Allied squadron came off well at first, losing only two of the destroyers and having *Exeter* damaged. Towards midnight, Doorman having ordered H.M.S. *Perth* and U.S.S. *Houston* to retire, covered their withdrawal by engaging the nearest Japanese squadron with *De Ruyter* and *Java*. As the two ships turned south meaning to cross in front of the Japanese ships, the Japanese Admiral thought they were withdrawing and ordered a torpedo attack. The cruisers *Haguro* and *Nachi*, and some destroyers launched a 'fan' of torpedoes at 8,000 yds range, and both the Dutch ships were torpedoed, *Java* sinking in 15 minutes with great loss of life. As a result of this battle Allied naval forces in the Java Sea area were almost completely wiped out.

46. Admiral Graf Spee: Armoured Ship, Germany

Admiral Graf Spee (the name was more commonly known as *Graf Spee* for short) was one of the first ships in World War 2 to make major headline news throughout the world. Her story is well-known, and she also brought into currency the term 'pocket battleship', a journalistic rather than a naval description. *Graf Spee* was not the first of her class, but she was the best known. The circumstances which brought the pocket battleship about were the restrictions of the

Versailles Treaty which limited the post-1919 Germany Navy to major units of no more than 10,000 tons displacement. In Washington Treaty terms this was regarded as the maximum tonnage for a cruiser, and the Washington Treaty signatories all built cruiser classes to conform. The German naval staff, however, with 10,000 tons as the top limit, determined to build something able to outclass a cruiser in firepower and armour and the result was a design which they called Panzerschiffe A (armoured ship A). This caused some alarm among other powers and as a direct result of this France pressed forward with the construction of the big battle-ships *Dunkerque* and *Strasbourg*, thus hastening the end of the Washington Treaty agreements. None the less, the German ships did not breach the limits of the Versailles Treaty – they merely exploited a loophole – and Germany was not a signatory to the Washington Treaty.

The Panzerschiffe A design was a considerable technical achievement for though no greater in tonnage and dimensions than a heavy cruiser, the German designers managed to lay on heavy armour protection, and provide a speed (26–28 knots), which was as good as most contemporary cruisers and faster than most battleships in service in the 1930s, as well as build in a heavy gun broadside of six 11 inch guns. The range of the ship exceeded 20,000 miles at 18 knots, an astonishingly high figure. All these characteristics were achieved by the most advanced technology of the time. Weight saving was clearly of great importance and this was achieved by welding throughout, instead of the riveted construction which was almost mandatory for warships in the 1930 period. Light metals and alloys were used wherever possible, and the then almost conventional warship propulsion by boilers and geared turbines was replaced by diesel engines. The diesel propulsion offered other useful features, besides saving weight and space. The ship could get underway very quickly, could accelerate quickly, and made virtually no smoke, all very advantageous for commerce raiding. The engines consisted of no less than eight MAN two-stroke diesels with a total power output of 56,000 hp, which in turn gave 26 knot top speed and up to 28 knots in favourable conditions. The engines drove two propeller shafts via reduction boxes. The design also featured roll stabilisers, a very early example of their use in warships.

First of the Panzerschiffe A vessels was *Deutschland* which started building in 1929 and was commissioned in April 1933. She was renamed *Lützow* in 1939 after her first operational sortie, allegedly as a precaution against the stigma of a ship with the *Deutschland* name being sunk in action. The second vessel was *Admiral Scheer*, laid down in June 1931 and commissioned in November 1934. *Graf Spee* was the last, laid down in October 1932 and commissioned in January 1936. The builder of *Graf Spee* was Wilhelmshaven Navy Yard. There were differences between each ship, *Deutschland* in particular having a simpler more rounded superstructure and conning tower. *Graf Spee* was 609¼ ft overall, 69½ ft in beam, and drew 21⅔ ft. While the standard displacement was nominally 10,000 tons, in practice this was exceeded, and the deep displacement was about 12,000 tons. The armament consisted of six 28 cm (6 inch) guns in two triple turrets, eight 15 cm (5·9 inch) in single mounts, and six 10·5 cm AA guns. There were eight 53 cm torpedo tubes in two quadruple mounts, one each side of the

after deck. There was provision for two seaplanes, the Arado 196 being in service by the outbreak of war. A catapult and two cranes served the aircraft, but the cranes were also used to hoist out boats. The armour protection was extensive, superior in *Graf Spee* to her sister ships in the light of operating experience. The deck armour was up to 45 mm thick, the turrets up to 140 mm thick, and the conning tower 150 mm. The hull armour was 60–80 mm thick, angled from the waterline, thus giving a greater effective thickness. Full length torpedo bulkheads were 40 mm thick. There were also 20 mm thick longitudinal bulkheads, and very complete compartmentalisation was intended to give a high degree of damage control integrity.

A particular distinction of *Graf Spee* (but not her sisters) was that in 1938 she became the first German warship to be fitted with what was then thought of as radio ranging – later called radar – and the early type of set had a distinctive 'bedstead' shape aerial high up on the foremast. There was also radio interception equipment to pick up radio transmissions from ships within range – this was put to good use in *Graf Spee*'s commerce-raiding activities in the opening months of the war.

The naval war plans called for an all-out war on British merchant shipping in the event that Britain became an enemy, and to this end some fine fleet supply ships had been built so that there was roughly one replenishment ship for every major surface vessel in the Kriegsmarine. The ships sent out as commerce raiders were to have supply vessels in designated areas with which they could rendezvous as required to refuel and re-store. Thus *Deutschland* operated in northern waters supported by *Westerwald*. *Graf Spee* was to be supported by *Altmark* and operated in the South Atlantic. *Graf Spee* left Wilhelmshaven on 21 August 1939. *Altmark* was already on station and the type of co-operation between the two ships is described under the story of *Altmark*. *Graf Spee* first struck on 30 September 1939, when she intercepted and sank the British ship *Clement*.

This set the Royal Navy off in search of the *Graf Spee* and several scouting groups were sent to the South Atlantic to seek out the German ships. On 5 October 1939, *Graf Spee* captured the British freighter *Newton Beech* intact and found useful intel-

ligence about British steamer routes and procedures. *Newton Beech* was kept as a prize to hold captured seamen. Two days later the steamer *Ashlea* was sunk, and *Newton Beech* was sunk also as her slow speed was becoming a liability. Three days later another steamer *Huntsman* was taken as a prize. On the next *Altmark* rendezvous *Graf Spee* transferred the captured British seamen to the supply ship, then took all worthwhile stores from *Huntsman* before sinking her. *Graf Spee* then steamed south in the direction of the Cape heading towards the Indian Ocean. En route the freighter *Trevanion* was sunk and *Graf Spee* retraced the route back towards the Atlantic but as there was the threat of an Anglo-French hunt-force coming south, the German ship headed out into the Indian Ocean at the end of October.

The pickings off the southeast coast of Africa proved poor, however, with only one small tanker, *Africa Shell*, sunk on 15 November 1939. The crew were allowed to row ashore, the *Graf Spee*'s captain intending them to raise the alarm as a diversion while he slipped back into the Atlantic. Another rendezvous was made with *Altmark* after which a week was spent on maintenance work, the engines in particular now showing the strain of the ship's long cruise. The ship sailed north-west and then intercepted the 10,000 ton freighter *Doric Star* between Cape Town and Freetown. This proved to be a fatal mistake, for *Graf Spee* stopped her victim by gunfire at extreme range, and this gave *Doric Star* time enough to transmit her position and the fact that her attacker was a battleship.

Graf Spee now steamed south-west towards South America and captured and sank another steamer, *Tairoa*. This ship was also able to transmit a position before she was sunk and from this it was possible for the British Commodore Henry Harwood, commanding the South American Squadron, to deduce that *Graf Spee* was heading for the River Plate area. Harwood moved his three cruisers, *Exeter*, *Ajax*, and *Achilles* to this area. En route to the South American coast, *Graf Spee* sighted and sank yet another steamer. From documentary evidence captured on the steamer, plus radio reports from Germany, the captain of *Graf Spee* was led to believe that several British ships were likely to leave Montevideo shortly and would make excellent prizes.

Off the River Plate on 13 December 1939, the *Graf Spee* spotted the masts and smoke of three ships which her commander Captain Langsdorff took to be merchant ships on convoy. On closing, however, the ships proved to be the British cruiser squadron. By pre-arranged plan, *Exeter* engaged *Graf Spee* direct while *Ajax* and *Achilles* worked round to engage from opposite directions. *Exeter* took the brunt of *Graf Spee*'s broadside and her forward turrets were put out of action and much other damage was done. *Exeter* made an unsuccessful torpedo attack and then withdrew from the action unable to continue the fight. *Ajax* and *Achilles* made torpedo attacks and her after turrets were put out of action by hits from *Graf Spee*'s 11 inch guns. By this time the British ships were sustaining much damage and withdrew under a smokescreen. *Graf Spee* had been holed and damaged, and entered Montevideo harbour to effect repairs. Captain Langsdorff requested a 14 day stay, but the Uruguay government would allow only 72 hours. Some thirty-six members of *Graf Spee*'s crew had been killed in the action and were buried ashore.

Graf Spee was now short of ammunition, had insufficient

time allowed for repairs, and there was the certainty that further British ships would be heading for the River Plate to await *Graf Spee*'s departure. Captain Langsdorff had to face the fact that a superior British force would almost certainly destroy *Graf Spee* as soon as she left territorial waters. Langsdorff therefore decided to scuttle his ship by blowing up the remainder of the ammunition; the *Graf Spee* therefore steamed out into the roadsteads and anchored. Her crew were taken off and the ship blew up, the time just after 1900 hours on 18 December 1939. The crew were interned and two days later Captain Langsdorff shot himself, an unfortunate end to a skilful operational cruise on the part of *Graf Spee* and her captain. In only two months *Graf Spee* had sunk nine British merchant ships, in itself no great total, but her elusiveness and daring had afforded great psychological warfare value to the Germans in the opening months of the war.

47/48. **Alisma/Surprise:** Corvettes, U.K./U.S.A.

The 'Flower' class corvettes were among the most famous of all the British-built warships of World War 2. Over 250 were constructed in both British and Canadian yards and they came at a time when Britain was badly depleted of escort ships, much needed to escort the convoys. Planning to build escort ships in large numbers began in 1938 when war seemed imminent and shipbuilding facilities would be stretched. Because non-naval yards would have to do the building, extreme simplicity was necessary and construction would have to be within the capability of all commercial builders. The new design had to be extremely seaworthy for deep ocean work and yet be quick to produce.

To meet all these requirements the Admiralty decided to adapt the most suitable type of mercantile vessel to hand, and the answer was found in the whale catcher *Southern Pride* which was built by Smiths' Dock Co. and designed by the chief executive of that firm. First thoughts were that the new naval type would have to be suitable for both minesweeping and anti-submarine work, operating mainly in the North Sea and Channel. While the design was being perfected, however, it was seen that the major requirement would be for service in the Atlantic and Western Approaches. As it turned out, the 'Flower' class served everywhere. To keep maintenance and operation simple, triple expansion reciprocating engines were used, with a single screw. The *Southern Pride* design was followed very closely except that the fo'c'sle was built up to take a single 4 inch gun, and the aft superstructure was eliminated to give a clear after deck for depth charge racks, chutes, and throwers. The design was quickly finalised and the first orders were placed in the summer of 1939.

The name 'corvette' was given to the new class of vessel which was unlike previous naval types in many ways. This was more distinctive than 'patrol vessel' and other designations first considered. Once construction got under way the ships were built at a great rate, and by 1941 as many as eight corvettes a month were being completed. The minesweeping requirement was dropped, though a few ships were, in fact, fitted for sweeping in the early days. The early ships had a short fo'c'sle, ending forward of the bridge, and this feature, together with a pole foremast ahead of the bridge, and a wood bridge and wheelhouse, betrayed the

mercantile origin of the design. Very soon, however, numerous modifications were made to better suit the ships for operations. Most noticeably the fo'c'sle deck level was extended well aft, breaking by the funnel, and this not only improved the sea-keeping capability, but also gave much needed extra accommodation; for as radar was fitted, plus more guns and depth charges, so did the number of crew members increase, from twenty-nine as originally planned up to over eighty. An open naval type steel bridge with an 'Asdic house', and the mast moved aft of the bridge were other major changes. Another very characteristic feature was the prominent lantern' which actually housed the Type 271 radar aerial. This radar set was fitted to virtually all the ships of the class and played a vital part in the anti-submarine war no less than Asdic and depth charges, for the radar could pick up surfaced U-Boats.

The armament was originally one 4 inch gun forward and a single 2 pdr pom-pom aft of the funnel. On the early units there were twin depth charge rails aft and two throwers, but two extra throwers were soon fitted and from late 1941 onwards many ships had a Hedgehog bomb thrower on the fo'c'sle deck starboard side. As more guns became available two or four Oerlikons were added in many ships, but there was great variety in this respect. After 135 ships had been built to original contracts a slightly altered type, known as the 'Modified Flowers' appeared. In essence these were ships built from the start with all the improvements noted above. Ships built to the later standards started to appear from late 1942. 'Flower' class corvettes served with the Royal Navy, U.S. Navy, Royal Canadian Navy, Netherlands, Norwegian, Free French (see *Aconit*), Danish, Greek, Venezuelan, New Zealand, Indian, Dominican, Argentine, Chilean and Yugoslav Navies, either during or just after World War 2, and then war surplus ships went to many other navies in the 1950s.

In service it was soon found that the 'Flowers' had their limitations, particularly in Atlantic weather, and for this reason larger, faster, longer ranged types like the 'River' class frigates were built. However, the later bigger ships never supplanted the 'Flowers' in service, and 'Flower' class ships were still being built until late 1944, vast numbers of them from

Canadian yards as well as from British yards.

'Flower' class corvettes were 205 ft long overall, 33 ft in beam, and drew $11\frac{1}{2}$ ft. The 'Modified Flowers' were $208\frac{1}{4}$ ft overall. The standard displacement was 925 tons (980 in the later ships). The single shaft four cylinder reciprocating engine gave 2,750 hp, a top speed of 16 knots. The armament varied as described above. Ships supplied to the U.S. Navy (some eighteen in all) were in most cases refitted with a 3 inch gun replacing the 4 inch gun and sometimes had American radar fitted to suit them better for U.S. Navy service. Relatively few Royal Navy ships were supplied to the U.S. Navy under 'Reverse' Lease-Lend, but the ubiquitous 'Flowers' were among them. Some of the U.S. ships had a second 3 inch gun added aft.

With so many 'Flowers' built it is almost impossible to pick out any particular ship. The two illustrations show H.M.S. *Alisma*, a Royal Navy ship as she appeared in 1943 in the so-called Western Approaches camouflage scheme. She was one of the earlier ships, built by Harland and Wolff, Belfast, and launched in December 1940. She has the short fo'c'sle, but a modified bridge and radar. U.S.S. *Surprise* was one of the earliest Canadian-built ships (Crown Shipyard, summer 1940) but is shown as in mid-1944 modified to the fullest standard with long fo'c'sle, open steel bridge, extra guns and depth charge stowage, and, in this case, U.S. Navy radar and boats. She is in U.S. Navy MEASURE 16 (Thayer Scheme) camouflage, equivalent to the R.N. Western Approaches Scheme. *Surprise* was originally H.M.S. *Heliotrope* before transfer to the U.S. Navy.

49. **West Point:** Troopship, U.S.A.

Large numbers of peace-time liners were taken over by the U.S. Navy and Royal Navy during World War 2 to act as troop transports for the movement of the great armies of men engaged in land operations. In addition to the troop transport role, some other liners were used by the British and French as armed merchant cruisers (see *Jervis Bay*) in the early part of the war. Others became depot or accommodation ships, and some were made into hospital ships. Yet others were more fully converted, notably by the U.S.N. and R.N.,

as large landing ships, carrying assault landing craft from davits so that troops could be landed in an amphibious assault. Aside from the naval authorities, other users of troopships were the U.S. Navy and the British Ministry of War Transport. In fact virtually all British troopships were mercantile manned, including the two famous 'Queens', *Queen Mary* and *Queen Elizabeth*.

The major passenger liners like the 'Queens' usually had speed enough to operate independently since at over 30 knots they were generally too fast for interception by submarine. In one incident *Queen Mary* sank a British cruiser by slicing it in half at top speed, but it was sometime before the accident was realised. Apart from donning a suitable paint scheme, extra life rafts, radar, and sometimes some light AA guns, the ex-liners used as troopships on ocean routes were little changed from their peace-time appearance. The typical vessel shown is *West Point*, renamed from her better known name of *America*, flagship of the United States Lines, when first completed in 1939. In June 1941 she became a troopship until 1946. She was a 23,179 tons gross vessel and could carry several thousand troops. The illustration shows her as in 1943, painted in a light disruptive scheme for the North Atlantic route, which was known as MEASURE 33.

50/51. Rockingham/Reuben James: Destroyers, U.S./U.K.

The U.S. Navy 'four stacker' destroyers were legendary vessels, actually relics of World War 1, 272 having been built in the 1918–22 period. Relatively few of them actually saw war service before the 1918 armistice, and by 1940 over 100 had been scrapped (some of these being wrecked in service) and the bulk of the survivors were in reserve, technically over-age. None the less, as the U.S. Navy had not started building destroyers again until the 1930s, then in small numbers, the 'four stackers' still formed a large proportion of the destroyer force in December 1941 when America entered World War 2. The ships were built originally as part of the 1917 re-armament drive and they were designed for rapid construction by the major ship-yards like Bethlehem Steel and Bath Iron Works. Many of the parts were pre-fabricated and the building schedule was tight.

One ship, *Ward*, was built by Mare Island Navy Yard in only 17 days from an empty slip to launching.

There were actually several slightly different designs, all superficially similar but dependent on the builder for the actual sub-type. One of the variants actually had only three funnels. Two boiler rooms each with two boilers gave rise to the distinctive funnel layout. In some ships – such as those converted to sea-plane tenders – the forward boilers and funnels were removed, giving an even odder appearance to ships so altered. The ships were $314\frac{1}{2}$ ft long overall, 310 ft at waterline, with $31\frac{3}{4}$ ft beam, and drawing $8\frac{3}{4}$ ft. Two shaft geared turbines gave 26,000 shp for a top speed of 35 knots. The displacement was 1,090 tons or 1,190 tons standard depending on sub-type. The crew was 150 and the original armament was four 4 inch guns, one 3 inch gun and twelve 21 inch torpedo tubes in four triple banks. The ships were very sleek and narrow which made them notoriously lively in rough weather.

By 1940 they were distinctly 'over-age' by any standard, yet they went on to give arduous and heroic war service under all sorts of conditions and they did everything from convoy escort work to gunfire support for landings. Some were converted to fast troop transports, others to seaplane tenders, some did experimental work, and a large batch became fast minesweepers. The 'four stackers' became famous the world over when fifty of them were transferred from the U.S. Navy to the Royal Navy in September 1940, following the historic 'ships for bases' deal between President Roosevelt and Prime Minister Churchill. At this time the Royal Navy was desperately short of destroyers – due to war losses – and needed more convoy escorts. Fifty of the 'four stackers' were stored up and steamed to Halifax where Royal Navy crews took them to Britain.

In British service there were usually a number of changes. The armament was reduced and altered to improve stability (less topweight) and the torpedo tubes were mostly removed. Many ships had the bridges altered to British style or plated in, and the distinctive Type 271 search radar aerial was added to most of them. Cutting down the funnel tops was also done to reduce top weight. The most famous of the British ships was undoubtedly *Campbeltown* which, laden with explosives, was used to ram the big dock gates at St. Nazaire in the daring commando raid of March 1942. This denied the use of the St. Nazaire docks to the Germans for repair of the biggest battleships. Some of the fifty ships were manned by the Royal Canadian Navy. Nine of the British ships were handed over to the Soviet Navy in 1944, while others served with Norwegian and Polish naval crews. One ship, *Stewart*, was captured in drydock when the Japanese took Surabaya, Java, in early 1942, and she was repaired and put back into service with the Japanese Navy.

With so many ships giving distinguished service it is difficult to pick out specific vessels. However, one illustration shows *Reuben James* (DD.245) which had the distinction of being the first U.S. Navy ship sunk in World War 2. This was on 31 October 1941, before America was officially in the war either against Japan or Germany. President Roosevelt had declared a 'short of war' policy in 1940 whereby U.S. ships would patrol a Neutrality Zone off the U.S. East Coast to prevent acts of war and would also help escort convoys within range of U.S.

ports. *Reuben James* was escorting a British convoy to the west of Iceland when she was torpedoed by a U-Boat with the loss of 100 of her crew. The interesting colour scheme was an early version of the MEASURE 2 low visibility scheme of navy blue, ocean gray, and haze gray which was altered to a simpler more formal style in later years. *Reuben James* was built by New York Shipbuilding Co.

The other illustration shows H.M.S. *Rockingham*, one of the fifty R.N. ships with the alterations made to suit these vessels as convoy escorts. She is in the Western Approaches colour scheme, has five 20 mm Oerlikon guns, retains only one 4 inch and the one 3 inch gun, retains one set of torpedo tubes, has search radar fitted, and cut down after funnels. She was built by Bethlehem Steel (Quantum). She sunk after hitting a mine in September 1944.

52/53. Long Island/Ameer: Escort Carriers, U.S.A./U.K.

Like the corvette, the escort carrier (also known as 'baby flat tops' or 'Woolworth carriers') was very much a stop-gap design, arrived at with a combination of necessity and ingenuity. Also, like the corvette, the escort carrier was part of the war against the submarine, but the concept started off more importantly as a way of giving air protection to the convoy. For when Germany had occupied most of Europe by mid-1940, airfields in France could put Atlantic convoys in reach of the four motor Focke Wulf aircraft. This type rarely attacked a convoy, but by shadowing it at a safe distance it could 'home' U-Boats to the area. An initial method of carrying a fighter plane to eliminate the Condor was to fit a catapult and an over-age Hurricane fighter to a suitable merchant ship. This was not wholly satisfactory for the Hurricane was expended after each sortie, being out of range of land; the pilot had to bale out or ditch the aircraft and be recovered by the parent ship.

A better idea was to put a short flight deck on the hull of a merchant ship so that aircraft could take off and land. The ship itself carried cargo and up to six aircraft might be carried and parked on deck. The first R.N. ship of this sort was H.M.S. *Audacity*, converted from a captured German freighter. *Audacity* had a short active life and was sunk while escorting a convoy across the Bay of Biscay in December 1941. But she had already proved the value of the escort carrier concept. A few other escort carriers were built in Britain, but it was America, with vaster shipbuilding resources, which now took over and developed the concept on a grand scale.

The U.S. Navy followed *Audacity* within weeks by converting two Moore-MacCormack Line freighters, *Mormacmail* and *Mormacland* into 'auxiliary aircraft carriers'. The first of these was renamed *Long Island* and the second, *Archer*, and this latter was handed straight over to the Royal Navy on completion in November 1941. *Long Island* commissioned into the U.S. Navy at the same time. These ships were small by carrier standards – 492 ft overall, 69½ ft in beam, and 25¾ ft in draught, and 102 ft over flight deck width. The flight deck was a simple plank structure on a girder support built over the normal hull. The hangar below the flight deck was half length only. There was no bridge in *Long Island* (just deck edge control positions) though *Archer* differed in having a rudimentary bridge. In 1943 the designation of this type of ship

was changed to escort carrier (CVE) and *Long Island* was CVE.1. *Long Island* saw little combat service but she played an important role in training and development work for the scores of CVEs that followed. She was also used sometimes as an aircraft transport. The displacement of this ship was 11,300 tons and her single diesel motor of 8,500 shp gave a speed of 18 knots. She had a single 5 inch gun aft, two 3 inch guns forward, and could carry about twenty aircraft. The illustration shows her in 1944 in the 'crazy quilt' camouflage pattern of MEASURE 32.

The escort carrier design was swiftly improved upon. A complete class, the 'Bogues', were put in hand for rapid production in 1942, utilising the standard C3 cargo ship hull and following the style of *Long Island* and *Archer*. Some twenty-six of the 'Bogue' class were transferred to the Royal Navy, one group with diesel engines, but the bulk with geared turbines and a single shaft, giving 8,500 shp and 17 knots speed. These ships were 492 ft long overall, 69½ ft in beam and drawing 25½ ft, and of 11,420 tons displacement.

Ameer was one of the later ships, being launched in October

1942 and commissioned in May 1943. Built by the Seattle-Tacoma Shipbuilding Co., she sailed for Halifax, then escorted a convoy from Halifax to the Clyde. Typically she was not deployed in the convoy escort role for by that period there were plenty of escort carriers available and several were now deployed as assault carriers mainly with fighters for offensive operations in support of amphibious landings or against shore targets. *Ameer* went to the East Indies fleet for the offensive operations role though she was also used on occasion as an aircraft transport. She was in support of the landings at Arakan, January/February 1945. In April 1945 her Hellcats shot down the first Japanese aircraft to be claimed by British escort carrier aircraft. In July 1945 *Ameer* foiled an attempted Kamikaze attack, shooting down the Japanese plane before it hit her.

The illustration shows her as in May 1944 in an Admiralty Medium Disruptive scheme painted in equivalent U.S. Navy colours, and therefore not dissimilar to the MEASURE 22 of the U.S. Navy. In R.N. service the Lease-Lend CVEs were given some modification internally, mainly to fuel stowage and sup-ply, consequent to some bad fire accidents in earlier ships. A full length hangar was a feature of all but the early CVEs. *Ameer* had two 4 inch guns, sixteen 40 mm AA guns, and twenty 20 mm guns. She carried eighteen–twenty-four aircraft (Corsairs and Avengers in 1944) and had a crew of about 640.

54. Howe: Battleship, U.K.

H.M.S. *Howe* was one of the later sister ships of the ill-fated *Prince of Wales*. While built to the same design, she differed slightly in armament details, due to experience with the first two ships, *Prince of Wales* and *King George V*. The unrotating projectiles (rockets) were never fitted to *Howe* and the AA armament was better. When first built she had six eight-barrel 2 pdr pom-pom mounts, later increased to eight, and there were at one time nearly sixty Oerlikon 20 mm close range guns fitted. *Howe* was laid down in June 1937, launched in April 1940, and commissioned in August 1942, the builder being Fairfield Yard on the Clyde. Her early work was in screening Russian convoys, but in March 1943 she joined Force H in the

Mediterranean and was covering the invasion of Sicily. In September 1943 when the Italians surrendered, *Howe* took over Taranto harbour, a major Italian fleet anchorage. In June 1944 she sailed for the East Indies Fleet, and the illustration shows her as she appeared at this time. In December 1944 she moved to the newly formed British Pacific Fleet (Task Force 57) and was for a time the flagship. In the spring of 1945 she took part in the Okinawa operations, and she finally returned to Britain in 1946. After some years as a training ship she went into reserve and was stricken from the active list in 1957.

Details were the same as those for *Prince of Wales*. The illustration shows *Howe* in an Admiralty Dark Disruptive scheme.

55/56. **PT. 139/PT. 77**: Motor Torpedo Boats, U.S.A.

All the major navies built up varying fleets of small coastal type offensive vessels, and the motor gunboats, motor torpedo boats and similar types attracted a good deal of attention during World War 2. Britain and other nations had developed coastal motor boats in World War 1, fast vessels with petrol engine propulsion. In the interwar period there was much less effort in this field, though Russia, Italy, and Germany all built fast motor vessels in the 1930s. Britain built some experimental prototypes in the later 1930s from which the big output of British coastal forces was developed during the war years. U.S. development was based in part on 'private venture' prototypes purchased from a British firm. The Elco firm (Electric Boat Co.) built a production batch of MTBs (PT boats in the U.S. Navy designator code) in 1941–42 and from these a more or less standard hull form and layout was derived which was common to most subsequent U.S. production.

The two main designs were Elco 80 ft and Higgins 78 ft. The Higgins design had a length of 78 ft, beam of 20¾ ft, and drew 5¼ ft. Twin shaft gasoline engines of 4,500 hp gave a top speed of just over 40 knots. Four 21 inch torpedo tubes, one 40 mm and two 20 mm Oerlikons (one each side of the bridge) were the usual armaments but there were variations. Some boats had only two tubes. *PT. 77* was of this type and is shown as first

184

seen in service in 1942 in the two tone grey of MEASURE 2 which was a common yard finish for new boats. Over 200 Higgins 78 ft boats were built and some were transferred under Lease-Lend terms to the Royal Navy, Soviet Navy and Yugoslavia (conversely the British Vosper 70 ft MTB design was adopted for the U.S. Navy and built in U.S. yards). *PT. 77* was sunk in the Pacific in 1943.

The main Elco design was 80 ft long, 20¾ ft in beam and drew 5 ft. This had three shafts driven by gasoline engines of 4,050 hp, with a 40 knot top speed. Four 21 inch torpedo tubes, one or two 20 mm Oerlikons, and twin machine guns formed the armament, but there were variations in this. Over 300 were built of which about fifty were supplied to the Soviet Navy under Lease-Lend terms. The crew was fourteen.

The PT boats fought many tough actions in the Pacific islands and South-West Pacific where they hid up in lairs and under overhanging jungle covers. Much attention was paid to camouflage to conceal boats from enemy reconnaissance. Camouflage officers attached to squadrons used much individual initiative in this. The Elco

80 ft boat, *PT. 139*, illustrated was with a squadron in 1942 which painted all its vessels in a bizarre 'zebra stripe' pattern designed to confuse enemy range-finders. Other equally unusual schemes were seen on PT boats. Deep green and brown (for jungle concealment), all black, all navy blue, and versions of 'big ship' disruptive patterns were to be seen on PT boats, as well as the standard greys in various applications.

57. **Richard Beitzen:** Destroyer, Germany

Because of the Versailles Treaty restrictions Germany could build only small torpedo boats of under 1,000 tons displacement in the 1920s. When rearmament in Germany began in the late 1930s, and the treaty was abrogated, the naval staff set out to produce new destroyers of high quality to match the biggest and fastest in the world – the pace-setters here being Japan and France. The first of these ships were the 'Leberecht Maass' class of sixteen ships, built in the 1937–39 period. Fourth of them was *Richard Beitzen*. Following the French and Japanese manner these ships displaced 2,200 tons, were 374 ft long, and 37 ft in beam. The powerful armament included five 5 inch guns – two mounted forward, three aft, and four 37 mm AA guns. Later in the war other light AA guns were added. There were eight torpedo tubes in two quadruple mounts. The twin shaft turbines gave 70,000 shp, and a top speed of 38 knots. Crew was 315 men.

Richard Beitzen is shown in the 1939 type colour scheme of the Kriegsmarine which in some ships included graphited funnels. Most of the class were committed to the invasion of Norway in April 1940, where despite their firepower and size no less than five of the sixteen were sunk by *Warspite* and her attendant destroyers in the two Narvik battles.

A subsequent class, the 'Narviks' were a slightly enlarged version with a higher freeboard forward, and improved armament layout in some ships.

58/59. Franklin/Hornet (II): Aircraft Carriers, U.S.A.

The backbone of the U.S. Navy's massive air striking power in the Pacific from 1942 onwards were the 'Essex' class attack carriers,

of which twenty-four were completed with a further eight cancelled when the war ended. The 'Essex' class ships incorporated all the lessons learned from the design of the preceding carriers of the 'Yorktown' class. An important conclusion arising from the experience of the first two 'Yorktown' class vessels – *Enterprise* and *Yorktown* – was that a larger ship was desirable so that not less than four full squadrons of fighter, dive bomber, torpedo bomber, and scouting aircraft could be embarked, making allowance for the larger aircraft designs of the next generation which were already being planned as part of America's rearmament programme in 1939–40. The 'Yorktown' class were a nominal 20,000 tons and the enlarged design would be 27,000 tons, and proportionately longer and wider. The enlarged size would also permit a more generous AA gun armament, a recognised inadequacy on the 'Yorktown' class. The Naval Expansion Act of 1938 allowed for two new carriers. To provide another unit quickly the first of the new ships was a 'repeat' model of the 'Yorktown' class, the *Hornet*, also featured in this book.

While she was being built detailed plans were worked out for the enlarged design. As soon as *Hornet* (CV.8) was launched from the Newport News Shipbuilding yard, Newport News, Virginia, her slipway was taken over for the first of the bigger carriers, *Essex* (CV.9). The month was December 1940. The 'Essex' class design repeated some of the features of the 'Yorktowns'. There was arrestor gear at each end of the flight deck (later removed forward) so that aircraft could land at either end. There was a catapult in the hangar deck to launch aircraft through a hangar side opening, though this was seldom used and was later removed. There was a flight deck catapult port side, and when the hangar catapult was deleted it was replaced by a starboard catapult on the flight deck.

The original 'Essex' class ships were 872 ft overall, 147½ ft in beam and 28½ ft in draught. The hull beam was 93 ft and the flight deck was 109 ft wide and 870 ft long. The displacement was 27,100 tons standard and 33,900 tons loaded. Four shaft geared turbines gave 150,000 shp, with a top speed of 33 knots. The armament was twelve 5 inch guns (four twin turrets on the flight deck and four single mounts), plus between forty-four and sixty-eight 40 mm Bofors guns in quad mounts. A varying number of 20 mm Oerlikon guns was later fitted. Capacity for eighty-three/one hundred aircraft depended on types in service. The original complement was 2,171 men but this later rose to about 3,500 as more radar and guns were installed. Construction followed the style described for *Hornet*, with a wood planked unarmoured flight deck. Some eleven ships were already under construction when Japan and America went to war, but the first ship, *Essex*, did not commission until December 1942 and through 1943–44 new ships arrived to make up the largest single class of attack carriers in the world.

After the tenth ship there was a slight modification of design which gave a longer bow with more AA guns, and the overall length became 888 ft. These later ships were popularly known as 'long hull Essex' class. *Ticonderoga* was the first of these, and all the later ships were built from the start with two flight deck catapults. A deck edge elevator was an innovation leaving the mid part of the flight deck unbroken and allowing even more space in the capacious hangar. As the older

187

U.S. carriers were sunk in the early part of the war, so new 'Essex' class ships took their famous names – thus there were 'Essex' class carriers called *Hornet*, *Wasp*, and *Lexington* – also *Shangri La* which had been the original code name of the first *Hornet*'s destination when she set off on the epic Tokyo raid. The last ship, *Oriskany*, did not commission until 1950, and she had an enclosed 'hurricane' bow, to which standard most of the earlier ships were converted in the 1950s and 1960s. Angled decks and other developments of the 1950s were also incorporated, changing the ship's appearance greatly. In the 1960s scrapping began, but three of these veteran ships remained in active U.S. Navy service in 1975. All the 'Essex' class ships gave valiant service in the Pacific war as the nucleus of the powerful carrier task forces which took the air war to Japan and her captured territories. It would be impossible to cover the operational histories of even two ships in this large class. The illustrations show two almost at random, both of the short hull type.

Franklin (CV.13) won particular fame as the ship the Japanese could not sink. She took part in several of the major oper-

ations in 1943–45, including Guam and Leyte Gulf, and she was an early victim of the Kamikaze suicide raids, being damaged by an attack near Luzon in November 1944. She was quickly repaired but then was severely damaged on 19 March 1945 in a dive bombing raid while she was operating 60 miles off the Japanese coast. Bombs penetrated the flight deck setting off hangar fires, and damaging the bridge. There were well over 1,000 casualties, 772 of them killed. As the aviation fuel ignited the ship disappeared under a pall of black smoke, but miraculously she stayed afloat, her flight deck twisted and destroyed. The cruiser *Santa Fé* came alongside to help her crew fight the fires and evacuate wounded. By a tremendous effort the fires were extinguished and the ship limped home under her own steam to Brooklyn Navy Yard. She is illustrated as she was just before the raid, painted in the utilitarian MEASURE 14, an overall ocean grey colour.

The second ship of the class shown is *Hornet* (*II*) (CV.12), the ship named for the valiant first *Hornet* and actually the fourth 'Essex' class built. She took part in the famous Marianas battle ('Turkey Shoot'), Leyte

Gulf, Iwo Jima, and Palau, avenging the loss of her forebear. *Hornet* is shown in October 1944 painted in the 'crazy quilt' dazzle of MEASURE 32, a disruptive scheme applied in various patterns to many ships of the class.

60/61. **U-47/U-96**: Submarines, Germany

The Type VII U-Boat was the most numerous of all the German U-Boat fleet, over 600 being built. U-47 was the first U-Boat to get world-wide prominence in World War 2, for this was the boat, whose commander was Lieutenant Gunther Prien, which penetrated the defences at Scapa Flow via Holm Sound on 13 October 1939, and sank the battleship *Royal Oak* with heavy loss of life. U-47 was a type VII B U-Boat with a displacement (surface) of 753 tons, and submerged displacement of 857 tons, length overall was 218 ft, with a beam of 20¼ ft and draught of 15½ ft. For surface running two shaft diesel motors of 2,800 shp gave a speed of 17¼ knots, and, when submerged, electric motors gave a speed of 8 knots. The surface range was 6,500 miles at 12 knots, and submerged was 80 miles at

4 knots. Five 21 inch torpedo tubes were fitted, four forward and one at the stern. The armament was one 3·5 inch gun forward, and one 20 mm gun aft of the conning tower, though there were variations of this in other boats of this type.

The Type VII boat was developed from the Finnish submarine *Vetehinen*, which was of German design, produced for Finland before any German submarine force had been allowed. The original Type VII was soon enlarged, producing the VII B and lengthened still further to arrive at the VII C, and later variants. Early experience showed the Type VII to be the best of the early U-Boats, and this led to considerable development of this model. U-47 had a comparatively short life after her *Royal Oak* glory. During the Battle of Narvik in April 1940 U-47 ran aground under water and was nearly lost. On 7 March 1941 she was sunk during an attack on an Atlantic convoy by the 'Flower' class corvettes *Arbutus* and *Camellia*. The U-47 was built by Germania Werft of Kiel.

The Type VII C was a further enlargement of the Type VII, the displacement being increased to 769 tons (surface) and 871 tons (submerged). The Type VII C was 220¼ ft long overall. Other details were as for the Type VII B. The Type VII C was the most favoured model of all and was not built until the end of 1944. There were many detail differences – some had an extra gun platform aft of the conning tower to hold an extra gun. Typical armament was one 3·5 inch gun forward, and two 20 mm guns. The Type VII C carried reload torpedoes, an innovation with this type. U-96 was one of the most successful of the Type VII C and under one commander, Lehmann-Willenrock, made a notable score of kills between 1940–42 in eight operational patrols with this boat against major Atlantic convoys. U-96 was sunk in March 1945.

62. **Prinz Eugen:** Heavy Cruiser, Germany

Prinz Eugen was one of the most famous of German warships, and was one of the few major German units to survive the war and remain unscathed and fully operational in 1945. The 'Hipper' class cruisers were built well outside the 10,000 tons limit of the Versailles Treaty, but by the time they were built in 1937–39, the Nazi regime in Germany had in any case abrogated the terms of the treaty. 'Hipper' class ships were exceptionally well armed and equipped, arguably the finest cruisers in the world when new. They were longer than many battleships in service elsewhere. There were considerable detail differences between the ships, *Prinz Eugen* being the best equipped of all.

Of her sisters, *Lützow* never saw service with the Kriegsmarine. Under the German–Soviet treaty over Poland, she was sold to the Soviet Navy and was in turn bombed and disabled at Leningrad by German aircraft when Germany invaded Russia. *Blücher* was sunk very early in her career, by gunfire and torpedoes from shore batteries in Oslofjord during the invasion of Norway in April 1940. *Admiral Hipper* was rammed and damaged by the British destroyer *Glow-worm* during operations off Norway in April 1940. She subsequently had a very active career in Arctic waters, the Barents Sea and the Baltic against Soviet forces. *Seydlitz* was to be converted to an aircraft carrier but work was not finished at the end of the war and she was scuttled incomplete. *Prinz Eugen* was associated originally with the battleship *Bismarck* for she was the battleship's consort on the first and only big occasion that *Bismarck* undertook. It was a shot from *Prinz Eugen* which started the first ammunition fire in *Hood* before she blew up.

Prinz Eugen was built by Germania Werft of Kiel and was launched on 22 August 1938. She did not commission until late 1940. The standard displacement was 16,230 tons, full load 18,400 tons. She was 654 ft overall, 71 ft in beam and drew 15 ft. A combination of four shaft geared turbines and diesels gave 132,000 shp and a top speed of 32 knots. She had a range of 6,800 miles at 18 knots. The main armament was eight 8 inch guns in four twin turrets, twelve 4·1 inch high angle guns in six twin turrets, and twelve 37 mm AA guns in six twin mounts. Initially she had eight, but later up to twenty-eight 20 mm AA guns. There were four triple 21 inch torpedo tubes and a capacity for three aircraft, with a catapult. The crew was about 1,600 officers and men. The armour protection included 5 inches on the main belt, 4 inches on the deck, 2 inches on the bridge and 5 inches on the

main turrets. A handsome clipper bow – a retrospective modification which delayed her completion – and a cowled funnel were characteristics which distinguished her from her sister ships. The clipper bow was incorporated to improve the sea-keeping qualities as experience with *Hipper* showed her to be very wet forward in rough weather.

After the early relative successes with commerce raiding, and a cruise early in 1941 by *Scharnhorst* and *Gneisenau* which was most successful, it was decided to unleash *Bismarck* and *Prinz Eugen* into the Atlantic on a similar cruise as these proved to be the only ships fully available – break-downs and damage thwarted a plan to sail a much bigger task force. *Prinz Eugen* sailed with *Bismarck* on 18 May 1941, and by the end of that month the two largest capital ships in the world, *Hood* and *Bismarck*, were both sunk, following the sequence of pursuit and destruction of the German battleship. *Prinz Eugen* escaped and returned to Brest. She had been damaged by a magnetic mine a month or so before the sortie with *Bismarck* and at Brest more permanent repairs were effected. At Brest *Prinz*

Eugen was 'bottled up' by the Allies with *Scharnhorst* and *Gneisenau*, and it was thought desirable to get these three important ships back to German waters. In a daring dash the three ships, with destroyer escort, broke out by running the gauntlet of British retaliation up the English Channel, in February 1942. Despite British air attacks the ships got through.

There was little chance to use major surface vessels again, however, due to the dominance and watchfulness of the Allies, and in early 1943 *Prinz Eugen* joined a squadron of other big ships to form a training squadron in the Baltic so that the ships and men would not lie idle and unexercised in port. The plan was that the ships would then be instantly available if the chance was seen for diversion to the Atlantic. In 1944, *Prinz Eugen* again saw action giving gunfire support to the Army ashore off the Russian coast. These were relatively quiet times, however, and when the war ended *Prinz Eugen* was surrendered to the Allies at Copenhagen in May 1945. She was handed over to the U.S. Navy as a prize and with a de-militarised German crew she was sailed to the U.S.A. Just a year or so after the war ended,

however, *Prinz Eugen* was deliberately damaged as a target vessel for the Bikini atomic bomb tests. The damaged ship was later scuttled at Kwajalein in November 1947.

The colour scheme shown is that carried by *Prinz Eugen* at the time of the 'Channel Dash' in 1942. Both before this and at the end of the war she was in plain light grey.

63. **Arkansas:** Battleship, U.S.A.

The oldest commissioned battleship in the U.S. fleet in World War 2 was *Arkansas*, which had been launched early in 1911. She had been with the U.S. Navy squadron attached to the Grand Fleet in the 1917–18 period. In those days she had the characteristic 'bird cage' masts of U.S. battleships but in the 1925–27 period she was modernised considerably. She was changed from coalfiring to oil fuel, had one funnel removed, and had the after cage mast replaced by a tripod mast. In 1941, before America went to war, *Arkansas* was in the powerful task force which escorted a garrison of U.S. troops to Iceland. Early in 1942 she underwent a further refit in which the forward cage mast was replaced by another tripod carrying the control tops, and the AA armament was augmented. From July 1942 *Arkansas* was flagship of Task Force 38, screening American troopship convoys from U.S.A. to Britain. The illustration shows her as she appeared at this time, in MEASURE 22 camouflage. At Normandy, *Arkansas* was in the fire support group with the Western Task Force and gave notable service off 'Omaha' beach. In late June 1944 the same group bombarded Cherbourg during the taking of the port. In August 1944 she took part in the preliminary bombardment for the Allied landings in the South of France.

With no more likely major landings in Europe, *Arkansas* was now sent to the Pacific and there she operated in the battleship force supporting the epic landings at Iwo Jima and Okinawa. The ship was finally sunk while acting as a target for the atomic bomb tests at Bikini Atoll in July 1946.

Arkansas was 562 ft long overall, 106¼ ft in beam and drew 26 ft. Four shaft geared turbines of 28,000 shp gave a top speed of 21 knots. Displacement was 26,100 tons standard. The armament at the end of World War 2 was twelve 12 inch guns in six twin turrets, six 5 inch guns, ten 3 inch guns, and thirty-six 40 mm Bofors guns. There was a crew of 1,650 officers and men.

64. **Augusta:** Heavy Cruiser, U.S.A.

The 'Northampton' class heavy cruisers were built to the Washington Treaty limitations of 10,000 tons and 8 inch turrets. First ships to meet the requirement were the 'Pensacola' class of two ships, and six ships of the 'Northampton' class were improved versions. *Augusta* of this class, like her sister ship *Houston* (lost at the Battle of the Java Sea), was built at Newport News Shipbuilding Co., Norfolk, Virginia. She was laid down on 2 July 1928, launched on 1 February 1930, and commissioned on 30 January 1931. She displaced 9,050 tons standard, 12,000 tons full load. She was 600 ¼ft in overall length, 66½ ft in beam and 16½ ft in draught. There was 3 inches of side armour, 1½ inches on the turrets, and 2 to 1 inch on decks. Four shaft geared turbines of 107,000 shp gave a top speed of 32½ knots. There were three triple 8 inch gun turrets, and eight single 5 inch mounts, but in World War 2 there was considerable addition of light AA guns, up to thirty-two 40 mm Bofors guns (eight quad mounts), and up to twenty-seven 20 mm Oerlikons. There were two midships catapults for aircraft, plus associated cranes. The crew in war-time totalled 1,100 officers and men.

Augusta was one of relatively few U.S. Navy ships to spend the whole of the World War 2 period in the Atlantic. In the summer of 1941 she was the flagship of the U.S. Alantic Fleet and as such she became well-known as the ship which carried President Roosevelt to Argentia, Newfoundland. Here he met Prime Minister Churchill who had been brought from Britain in the battleship *Prince of Wales*. This was the meeting which established the basis of the Atlantic Charter and the Lease-Lend scheme which provided much needed equipment for Britain and other Allies.

The illustration shows *Augusta* as she appeared at this time with an early application of what became the most common U.S. Navy colour scheme – MEASURE 22. White top masts and control tops were a refinement intended to reduce visibility when the ship was hull down. This was soon dropped with this particular colour scheme; radar, however, reduced the importance of visual sighting and ranging. In subsequent years *Augusta* saw much hard service. For Operation Torch, 8 November 1942, *Augusta* was one of the bombarding cruisers at Fedala, the centre attack area. On D-Day, the Normandy landings of 6 June 1944, *Augusta* was the flagship of Admiral Kirk the U.S. Navy commander, and took part in the bombardment. She was also at the taking of Cherbourg and then led the American naval forces in Operation Anvil, the landing in Southern France.

65. **Hood:** Battle-cruiser, U.K.

At the start of World War 2, H.M.S. *Hood* had the distinction of being the largest and most powerful warship in commission in the world, though this was being challenged by the new German battleships *Bismarck* and *Tirpitz*. For the whole inter-war period, however, *Hood* had stood as a symbol of Britain's naval might, unchallenged in size due to limitations in capital shipbuilding imposed by the Washington Treaty. *Hood* had been designed during World War I as the first of a proposed series of fast battle-cruisers of a size bigger than contemporary battleships. To achieve a 30 knot speed, however, the armour protection was somewhat lighter than that of a battleship and there was a considerable reduction in horizontal deck armour which was later to prove fatal.

As first built *Hood* displaced 41,200 tons at light load, was 860½ ft long overall, 105 ft in beam over the side bulges, and drew 28½ ft. Four shaft geared turbines of 144,000 shp were installed with a speed of 31 knots – though 32½ knots were achieved on trials. The armament was eight 15 inch guns in four turrets, twelve 5·5 inch guns, four 4 inch guns, four 3 pdr saluting guns, and six torpedo tubes. The side armour varied from 3 inches to 12 inches, the barbettes had 12 inches, turrets 11–15 inches, and conning tower 5–12 inches. Deck armour varied from ¾ inch, to 1½ inch, to 3 inches over magazines – very light, but decks were considered least vulnerable back in the 1916–20 period when *Hood* was planned and built.

In the last year of peace, *Hood* was scheduled to begin a major refit which would have modern-ised her in a similar fashion to *Renown*, *Warspite*, and *Queen Elizabeth*, and would have provided a new superstructure and up to date secondary armament. Had this work been undertaken the final appearance would have been something like a lengthened version of *Prince of Wales* or *Howe*, with the same secondary armament. Because war seemed most probable, however, this ambitious refit scheme was dropped and a very limited refit was done which included fitting four twin 4 inch AA mounts on the boat deck in place of four single 4 inch guns, and the associated control systems. An eight-barrel 2 pdr pom-pom mount was also fitted.

By the time war started in September 1939 she was at sea patrolling in the North Atlantic. In November 1939 she was part of a combined French–British Force, seeking out the German battle-cruisers *Scharnhorst* and *Gneisenau* – without success. The changes of the immediate pre-war refit caused trouble, in that displacement had been increased and the ship was now suffering from added stress in heavy weather. In March 1940 *Hood* went for another refit. All the 5·5 inch guns were removed and three more twin 4 inch mounts were added, as also were two more pom-pom mounts and five UP (unrotating projectiles) were fitted, one on B turret, and two each side on the boat deck. These UPs were parachute rockets and proved unsuccessful in general. After this refit, *Hood* covered the big convoy which brought Commonwealth troops to Britain in June 1940. *Hood* then sailed to the Mediterranean and became flagship of the newly-formed Force H. She was involved in the Mers-el-Kebir incident where the French fleet was largely destroyed to prevent its passing over to German use. In August 1940 she returned to Britain and was engaged in several patrols and searches in the North Sea and North Atlantic. A further refit took place in the first three months of 1941, including the fitting of radar. In March she returned to service and was once again off in search of *Scharnhorst* and *Gneisenau*.

In April 1941 came news that *Bismarck* was expected to sortie into the Atlantic, and *Hood* patrolled between Iceland and Scapa Flow. It was over a month before *Bismarck* appeared, and *Hood* and *Prince of Wales* were sent to Icelandic waters to cover the Denmark Strait. On 23 May 1941, *Bismarck* and *Prinz Eugen*

were sighted from the cruiser *Suffolk* and on the following day in the early hours *Hood* and *Prince of Wales* intercepted *Bismarck*. At 0549 hours they opened fire, and the German ships replied, a hit from *Prinz Eugen* starting a big fire from ready-use ammunition lockers on the boat deck. At 0555 hours *Hood* changed course slightly to bring her aft 15 inch gun turrets to bear, and as she did so a salvo from *Bismarck* hit her. A shell possibly went through the decks to the 4 inch magazines, though this was not necessarily the case. However, an explosion there set off the aft 15 inch magazines, and the resultant huge explosion blew the ship in half. The one fatal unremedied flaw in *Hood*'s design – the vulnerability from plunging fire – had apparently become the cause of her tragic end. It was Britain's greatest naval disaster of the war until that date and 1,418 officers and men were lost. There were just three survivors.

66. **Exeter:** Heavy Cruiser, U.K.

Graf Spee's main opponent at the Battle of the River Plate in December 1939 was the handsome British heavy cruiser *Exeter*. This ship was, like her contemporaries, built within the limits of the Washington Treaty. The major nations, including Britain, built 10,000 ton cruisers with 8 inch guns, the British efforts resulting in the three-funnel 'County' class of the late 1920s. These were expensive ships, however, and led to a decision to build a reduced size heavy cruiser below the 10,000 tons limit.

Thus were evolved two semi-sisters, *York* and *Exeter*, of 8,400 tons displacement and six 8 inch guns in three turrets. The overall length was 575 ft, beam 58 ft, draught 20 ft. The armament was six 8 inch guns, four 4 inch high angle guns and eight 21 inch torpedo tubes in two quad mounts. She had a 2–3 inch armoured belt and 2 inch deck armour. *York* differed from *Exeter* in having raked funnels and a taller more tower-like bridge. *Exeter* was given two catapults, one passing each side of the aft funnel and two aircraft were carried. This was a retrospective addition, after the ship had been commissioned in 1931.

Exeter was about to pay off from a commission in the South American station in August 1939, when she was ordered to sail again for the South Atlantic. With a hastily assembled squadron, *Exeter*, two 6 inch cruisers *Ajax* and *Achilles*, and *Cumberland*, Commodore Harwood in *Exeter* had to patrol the whole South American side of the South Atlantic from Rio de Janeiro to the Falkland Islands. In the opening months of the war the Panzerschiffe *Graf Spee* was operating in South Atlantic waters with some success and only narrowly escaped detection by *Cumberland* just a week after the war started. By early December *Graf Spee* had made her presence felt in no small way and it was possible from *Graf Spee*'s movements and sinkings to see that the German ship might be working across the Atlantic from the African coast to the South American coast. Harwood had changed his command ship from *Exeter* to *Ajax* to allow *Exeter* to sail south to the Falklands for a self-maintenance period. He held *Ajax* and *Achilles* near the entrance to the River Plate and recalled *Exeter*.

On 12 December 1939, the three ships were disposed off the River Plate and *Graf Spee* steamed into the trap the following day. Just after 1600 hours *Exeter* spotted smoke from *Graf Spee*'s funnel and was engaged by the German ship. In the action which followed *Exeter* came off badly, having her bridge damaged and put out of action. A and B turrets were put out of action and fires started between decks. *Exeter* herself hit *Graf Spee* three times. She withdrew from the action and returned to the Falkland Islands for repair, before returning to Plymouth. The sinking of *Graf Spee* was Britain's first great naval victory of the war, and the crews of *Ajax* and *Exeter* were given the Freedom of the City of London, and many decorations were awarded.

During 1940 the *Exeter* was refitted extensively with new masts, enlarged bridge, twin 4 inch guns replacing the single 4 inch guns, and two eight barrel pom-poms were added to the AA armament. In March 1941 *Exeter* recommissioned and sailed for the East Indies. After convoy and patrol work, war came to the East when Japan attacked Pearl Harbor in December 1941. When Singapore was attacked in February 1942, *Exeter* was part of the A.B.D.A. fleet which was operating off Surabaya in the Java Sea. Japanese cruisers and destroyers were encountered and in the ensuing battle *Exeter* was damaged in a boiler room and

returned to Surabaya for repairs. On 28 February 1942, with a British and American destroyer as escort, *Exeter* set off for Colombo, Ceylon. The small force ran into a Japanese fleet which included *Myoko* and *Haguro* and was severely pounded. *Exeter* was again hit in a boiler room which stopped her and left her a sitting target for the Japanese gunners. With shells now hitting her constantly her captain ordered the seacocks to be opened to sink her and the crew abandoned the ship.

67/68/69. **Inman/England/ Robert F. Keller:** Destroyer Escorts, U.K./U.S.A./U.S.A.

The type of ship designated as a destroyer escort was another unique warship designed to meet the new conditions of World War 2. DEs were originally intended to be built for supply under Lend-Lease to the British. As a result of deep ocean escort experience in the early convoys it was found that something bigger and longer ranged than 'Flower' class corvettes was needed. In Britain the 'River' class frigate resulted (also built in U.S.A. as 'Colony' class frigates). For a ship to be built in America, the Royal Navy asked for a length of 300 ft and a good range and speed. These stipulations aside, the design was to follow U.S. practice and requirements to ease production. Britain wanted fifty of the new DEs as a follow-up to the fifty 'over-age' destroyers she already had. This was soon increased to 250.

When the United States entered the war, she also had a requirement for DEs. As a result the bulk of the production was ultimately retained by the U.S. Navy and only eighty-four were supplied to Allied navies, including fifty-five to Britain. Some 1,005 DEs were ordered but at the war's end many were cancelled. None the less, some 563 were completed, making the DE one of the most numerous of all major size warships of World War 2. The design throughout was basically the same, but there were detail differences between the six groups produced conditioned by the availability of engines and armament requirements. To speed up output the early group, 'Evarts' class, had diesel motors of 6,000 hp giving a speed of 21 knots. These were known as 'short hull' type being 289½ ft overall, with a 35 ft beam and drawing 8¼ ft. Of

the output of these, thirty-three were delivered to the Royal Navy and H.M.S. *Inman* is typical of these. The illustration shows her in 1944 by which time she was wearing a plain light grey colour scheme for Atlantic escort service. This first group of DEs lacked torpedo tubes. *Inman* was the last of this group to be commissioned for British service, in January 1944. Three 3 inch guns, four 40 mm Bofors, and four or five 20 mm Oerlikons were the most common armament, but there was great variety. Several of the British DEs had 2 pdr pom-poms mounted in the extreme bow as 'bowchaser' weapons for attacking marauding S-boats in the North Sea and English Channel.

The second and largest group were the 'Buckley' class of which U.S.S. *England* (DE.635) was to become the most famous of all DEs and one of only two ships of this type to win a Presidential Unit Citation for distinguished war service. Of the 'Buckleys', some forty-six were transferred to the Royal Navy. Together with the 'short hull' 'Evarts' class ships, the British vessels were known as the 'Captains' class, all being named after distinguished R.N. commanding officers of Nelson's time. 'Buckley' class DEs had twin shaft turbo-electric drive of 12,000 shp, giving a top speed of 23½ knots. Basic armament was three 3 inch guns and six 40 mm guns (three twin mounts). Early ships of all classes had 1·1 inch quad machine guns instead of Bofors guns, while in later ships a varying number of extra 20 mm Oerlikons and 40 mm Bofors. A triple 21 inch torpedo mount was placed aft of the funnel but was not fitted in the British ships. A distinctive feature of the 'Buckleys' was the twin trunked funnel. Anti-submarine equipment included a Hedgehog bomb thrower aft of the No. 1 3 inch mount in all ships, plus twin depth charge chutes aft and eight depth charge throwers (K guns); the British ships had only four throwers.

England was built by the Bethlehem Shipbuilding yard in San Francisco, launched on 26 September 1943, and commissioned on 10 December 1943. Her opportunity of immortality came in the last 12 days of May 1944 when she was part of an anti-submarine group in the South-West Pacific. At this time the local Japanese naval commander had had a line of submarines placed in wait to the north-east of the Admiralty Islands to observe and report back any U.S. fleet movement north into the Pacific. A chance spotting of one of the submarines led the DE group to be sent in. *England* located and sank the submarine, I-16, and in successive days, sank another five boats, RO-106, RO-104, RO-116, RO-108, and RO-105, which removed the entire line of submarines, and became the top scoring DE of the U.S. Navy. In his battle report *England*'s captain, Lieut. Cdr. Walton B. Pendleton ended his account of the action with the apt claim: 'It seems that practice does make perfect.' *England* is shown as she appeared soon after this exploit with the six submarine kills displayed by 'hash marks' on the bridge sides along with her marks for shot down aircraft. The ship was in the plain ocean grey overall colour, MEASURE 14. Only 12 days after her great feat of submarine sinking, *England* was struck and slightly damaged by a Kamikaze attack, but on 9 May 1945, she received a direct hit by Kamikaze which caused considerable damage and set fire to the superstructure. She was saved, patched up, and towed back to Leyte Gulf, but she was too badly damaged to be worth full repair, so she was scrapped soon after the war ended.

A further group of DE, the 'Cannon' class, were diesel-electric powered, 306 ft overall, and 1,240 tons displacement. The twin diesel-electric drive of 6,000 shp gave a speed of 21 knots. Some of these were supplied under 'Lease-Lend' terms to France (see *Hova*, of this class) and others were supplied post-war to many nations including Greece, France, Holland, Brazil, Italy, China, Japan, Uruguay, and Peru. The 'Edsall' class were similar again, with geared diesel drive. The final two groups, 'Rudderow' and 'John C. Butler' were externally similar except that the former ships had twin turbo-electric drive and the latter had geared turbines. They differed from the previous classes by having two 5 inch guns replacing the 3 inch guns – one mount forward, one mount aft – and lower bridge and smokestack. The displacement went up to 1,450 tons. Most of these ships commissioned through 1944–45 and fewer of them had a chance to win great laurels. The ship shown, *Robert F. Keller*, is representative of one of these latter ships of the 'Rudderow' class. She was launched on 19 February 1944, and commissioned on 17 June 1944, the builders being Brown Shipbuilding Co., Houston. The illustration shows her in immediate post-war finish when U.S. Navy ships adopted an overall haze grey colour scheme, known as MEASURE 13. The large hull numbers of pre-war days were also used again.

70.   **Nicholas:**   Destroyer, U.S.A.

Between 1934 and 1940, America built several new classes of new destroyers as part of an Act of 1930 which provided a certain amount of armaments work to help relieve the depression. These ships followed European lines for the most part, with raised fo'c'sles and a tonnage of between 1,500 and 1,850. The ships were the first built since the 'four stackers' of World War 1 (see *Reuben James*). Meanwhile the Japanese, in particular, and the French, were building very large destroyers (see *Fubuki, Yukikaze, Le Fantasque*) which outmoded all existing U.S. destroyers in range and firepower. The 'Fletcher' class design was specifically intended to redress the balance and give the U.S. Navy a destroyer which matched those of its main potential enemy, Japan.

Gibbs and Cox, a New York firm of naval architects, drew up the plans. There was a reversion to a flush deck layout with high forward freeboard, the flush deck design being partly to simplify production. The structure was entirely welded and most of the eleven building yards which turned out 175 'Fletcher' class ships worked with sub-assemblies, so that vessels could be produced very quickly like 'Liberty' ships. Fastest building time from start to commissioning was 158 days – about five months – which was very fast work for a ship fitted with much sophisticated armament and electronics.

'Fletcher' class ships displaced 2,050 to 2,100 tons standard and 2,940 tons full load. Overall length was 376½ ft, the beam 39½ ft, and draught 17¾ ft. Two shaft geared turbines of 60,000 shp gave a top speed of about 36 knots. Two boiler rooms each held two boilers with an engine room adjacent to each boiler room. To minimise the chance of a hit in the boiler room rendering the ship immobile, each boiler could be used to drive either engine. Typical 'Fletcher' class armament comprised five 5 inch guns in single enclosed mounts. On early ships, like *Nicholas* when first built, the main AA armament was the quad 1·1 inch machine gun, but this was soon replaced by twin 40-mm Bofors and a varying number of 20 mm guns. Up to ten Bofors and 20 mm Oerlikon guns were mounted. There were two quintuple 21 inch torpedo mounts, and the crew numbered about 300. There were two depth charge racks aft and three depth charge mortars (known as K guns in the U.S. Navy) each side aft.

First contracts for 'Fletcher' class destroyers were placed late in 1940, and the keels were laid in the early part of 1941. *Nicholas* was launched at Bath Iron Works in February 1942 and commissioned on 4 June 1942. The illustration shows her when brand new in the common U.S. Navy MEASURE 12 colour scheme of the 1942 period. *Nicholas* saw busy war service. In October 1942 she led the escort to a badly needed convoy of aviation spirit, which had to be got through to Guadalcanal against continual Japanese air attack. In January 1943 she was in action with a force bombarding Munda and Vila, New Georgia, to deny Japanese forces the use of air strips at these points. In February 1943 *Nicholas* was part of a force intercepting the 'Tokyo Express' (a Japanese troopship convoy) at Guadalcanal. The destroyer force, known as 'Cactus', of which *Nicholas* was a part, carried out several further bombardments and interceptions in the New Georgia area in the weeks of the Guadalcanal campaign. In July 1943 *Nicholas* was involved in the Kula Gulf battle and picked up the survivors of the cruiser *Helena*. This was a major operation for a small destroyer and included the driving off and damaging of a Japanese destroyer (*Amigiri*) in the process. *Nicholas* was the flagship of Desron 21 at this time.

On 3 October 1943, she helped sink two landing craft and a gunboat at Bougainville. In February 1944 she was part of the force in the Gilbert Islands operation. For her excellent record she was awarded a Presidential Unit Citation and as if by celebration she sank the Japanese submarine, I-11 on 17 February 1944, while escorting a supply ship convoy to Kurajalein. This was a classic encounter where *Nicholas* made a radar contact while I-11 was on the surface, opened gunfire at a mile range, then made a thorough sonar search as the submarine submerged. In November 1944 she sank the I-37 in similar circumstances while screening a cruiser force near Ulithi. *Nicholas* was part of the destroyer force at the Borneo landings, and in August 1945 she led the destroyers which escorted *Missouri* into Tokyo Bay to accept the Japanese surrender, so ending a fine war record. *Nicholas* is illustrated when first commissioned in 1942.

71. **Nashville:** Heavy Cruiser, U.S.A.

Authorised under the 1934 programme, the 'Brooklyn' class of light cruiser heralded a new era of cruiser design for the U.S. Navy. The maximum Washington Treaty size of 10,000 tons was utilised to give a large platform for a big 6 inch gun armament. The previous layout with hangars and catapults amidships was dispensed with in favour of a clear flush deck, with hangars and catapults moved aft, so leaving more space for guns and large arcs of fire. Twin cranes aft and two catapults served the aircraft and there was room for six aircraft in a capacious stern hangar, though four floatplanes formed the usual complement. The relatively simple layout set the style for most subsequent cruiser and battleship classes.

There were no less than fifteen 6 inch guns, in five triple turrets. Turret number 2 super-fired above turrets 1 and 3. Secondary armament was eight single 5 inch guns, later replaced by four twin turrets in two of the ships. During the war years the light AA armament was supplemented to comprise twenty-eight 40 mm Bofors guns (seven quad mounts) and twenty-four or more 20 mm Oerlikons. The length overall was 608½ ft, 600 ft at the water-line, beam 61¾ ft, and draught 19½ ft. Four shaft geared tur-bines of 100,000 shp gave a top speed of 14 knots. Some ships of the class, including *Nashville*, had a slightly lower displace-ment, 9,745 tons. The crew was 1,300 officers and men. *Nashville* (CL.43) was the fourth to be built. New York Shipbuilding Co. were the constructors, and she was laid down in January 1935, launched on 2 October 1937 and commissioned in No-vember 1938. Despite the great size, these ships were 'light cruisers' in Washington Treaty terms, having 6 inch guns as main armament. The value of the large design was seen in the combat radius of 14,500 miles (at 15 knots) and the disposal of a larger number of guns than most contemporary cruisers.

Nashville was typical of the class of nine and saw distin-guished war service. In May 1942 she was flagship of the U.S.N. North Pacific Force which in-cluded two sister ships, *St. Louis* and *Honolulu*, two other cruisers and two destroyer divisions. The illustration shows the ship as she appeared at this time in the light disruptive camouflage pattern known as MEASURE 33. These were predominantly light colours for northerly latitudes. In June 1942 *Nashville* led the force in parrying off – not too success-fully – a Japanese attack on the West Aleutians which was mainly intended as a diversion from the attack on Midway. She fought at New Guinea and Leyte. Here, on 13 December 1944, *Nashville*, flagship of an attack task force, was hit by a Kamikaze raider, port side aft. 133 men were killed and 190 were wounded. In 1951 *Nashville* was transferred to the Chilean Navy as *Prat* and remained in service in 1975, forty years after being laid down.

SCHEMATIC CAMOUFLAGE PATTERNS

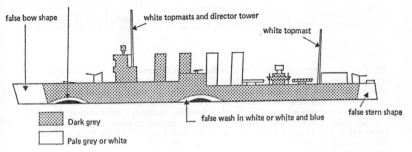

false bow wave in white or white and blue

false bow shape

white topmasts and director tower

white topmast

Dark grey

Pale grey or white

false wash in white or white and blue

false stern shape

Typical deceptive painting of a warship to show false bow and stern shapes and length, and false bow wave and wash. Four stack destroyer painted to resemble a two stack ship.

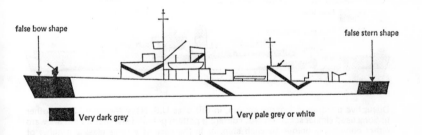

false bow shape

false stern shape

Very dark grey

Very pale grey or white

Variation on deceptive painting. Bow and stern painted out in a dark shade to 'merge' with the sea. Rest painted a light contrasting colour with pattern to cause optical confusion. German torpedo boat.

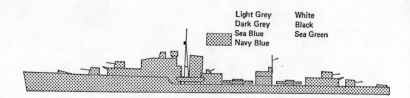

Light Grey
Dark Grey
Sea Blue
Navy Blue

White
Black
Sea Green

Solid colour schemes are not normally thought of as camouflage measures at all, but they have been proved the most effective for general conditions. Light greys of various shades represent the most favoured compromise in average conditions of weak sunlight and haze as a low visibility finish. In the Pacific in 1944–45 an overall Navy Blue was found very effective by the U.S. Navy for reducing visibility from the air, and the Japanese used a deep Sea Green for the same reason. Submarines have commonly been painted in very dark colours (black or dark grey) to reduce their underwater visibility from the air. Royal Navy submarines in World War 2 were sometimes painted a deep Sea Blue (Mediterranean) or deep Sea Green (Far East) for the same reason, these seas having more clarity from the air.

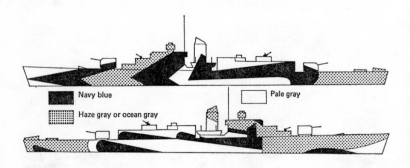

Navy blue

Pale gray

Haze gray or ocean gray

Disruptive painting in 'dazzle' pattern, in this case U.S. Navy Measure 32, but other nations used similar schemes. Note differing pattern port and starboard. Patterns were either completely unique to each ship, or in the case of a large class a number of different patterns were used and repeated through the class.

206

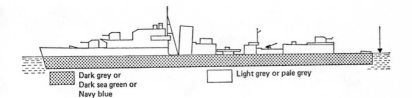

Dark grey or
Dark sea green or
Navy blue

Light grey or pale grey

Graded system of deceptive painting, used in various forms by nearly all navies. In this case the Admiralty Alternative Scheme on a British destroyer is shown but other nations (e.g., U.S., Navy Measure 22) used similar principle. The dark lower hull colour 'merged' with the sea and horizon line making distance difficult to judge.

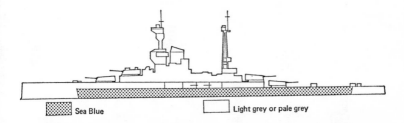

Sea Blue

Light grey or pale grey

Another deceptive scheme, used by the Royal Navy in the latter part of the war. The hull panel foreshortened the apparent length of the ship. At an extreme range the light grey might tend to 'merge' with the sky and the dark 'ship' shape of the hull panel might mislead the observer into wrongly identifying the type of ship. At very close range it could also give the impression of another smaller ship alongside. This was the Admiralty Light Standard Scheme of 1944–45, shown on a battleship. It was easy to apply and a good compromise scheme suitable for all sizes of warship.

207

INDEX

Ships are listed alphabetically by name, followed by country of origin or service, and type.